A Glimpse of Nothingness

Also by Janwillem van de Wetering

A Glimpse of Nothingness

Experiences in an American Zen Community

Janwillem van de Wetering

ST. MARTIN'S GRIFFIN

NEW YORK

THOMAS DUNNE BOOKS.
An imprint of St. Martin's Press.

A GLIMPSE OF NOTHINGNESS. Copyright © 1975 by Janwillem van de Wetering.
All rights reserved. Printed in the United States of America. No part of this
book may be used or reproduced in any manner whatsoever without written
permission except in the case of brief quotations embodied in critical articles or
reviews. For information, address St. Martin's Press, 175 Fifth Avenue,
New York, N.Y. 10010.

ISBN 0-312-20945-2

First published in Amsterdam under the title *Het Dagende Niets* by De Driehock

First published in the United States
by Houghton Mifflin Company

First St. Martin's Griffin Edition: May 1999

10 9 8 7 6 5 4 3 2 1

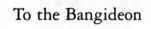
To the Bangideon

Preface

This book, like my first, *The Empty Mirror*, describes an authentic experience.

I changed the setting, to protect the Zen settlement from the curious. I also changed the names of the characters in the story. In fact, I chopped and combined so much that it will be strange indeed if anyone recognizes himself. I couldn't change the master but he won't recognize himself as he won't read the book. Who the master really is I wouldn't know. I could only describe his mask and costume and repeat some of the statements he made and try to recapture the sense of the conversations he had with me.

This is my last book on Buddhism. Whether any of the anecdotes, thoughts and conclusions appearing in this book are really Buddhist I couldn't say. The teaching is deep, I have scratched the surface. I hope I scratched right.

Contents

A Glimpse of Nothingness

One

Bubonic plague

A waiting room at a New York airport. A shed, rather. I had travelled cheaply, with a charter company, at a much reduced price. The plane hadn't been full. The company was begging for passengers. An inexperienced charter company, the entire trip had been characterized by mix-ups and slowdowns.

We had already spent hours under the corrugated iron roof of the shed. It wasn't just hot, it was clammy. There were no chairs but low wooden benches, as in an old-fashioned school, placed along the walls. A few children were crying. Women, with puffed up faces, complained, and men with loosened ties and red necks were running to and fro, trying, vainly, to arrange something.

We were waiting for immigration and customs who were supposed to come to us from the other side of the airport.

The establishment was temporarily represented by a fat black policeman, whose large revolver was loosely stuck into its holster, and who observed us pleasantly, in an indifferent manner.

The loudspeakers, hung in the four corners of the ceiling, addressed us croakingly, at regular intervals. As soon as the mechanical voice introduced itself in a nasty, hoarse, and loud whisper the passengers panicked. Almost everyone jumped up and rushed towards the luggage. The women pushed their way through, using elbows, till they were close to the policeman, whose expression never changed, and the men lumped together while children shouted and wailed, trying to stay close to their parents.

The passengers glared at the ceiling and sat down again. They mumbled and lit cigarettes. They lined up at the lemonade and coffee dispensers which, after a while, were sold out. Most of them were out of order anyway, saying so on crumpled bits of carton stuck to the glass with sticky tape.

I had found a corner, as far away as possible from the luggage.

The loudspeakers croaked again and the automatic bustle followed, perhaps for the tenth time. I looked at the few passengers who hadn't joined the crowd.

There was a young couple, perhaps on their honeymoon. They held hands and smiled. An old man, perhaps a grandfather on a family visit, sat on the same bench. His small suitcase protected his back against the hard wall. His eyes were closed but he wasn't asleep. His forehead was moist with sweat, but I saw no irritation on his face. A woman, some thirty years old, was sitting in a corner, not a pretty woman, with a bitter mouth. She didn't look up when the loudspeakers addressed her.

Love, a sense of relativity, indifference: three feelings to protect us against bustle and panic, murder and slaughter, against the tentacles of the "I" which, according to Buddhism, does not exist, doesn't exist in reality, but which does have an apparent identity, through which it can act.

I began to feel very stifled. At first I had read, then slept, uneasily and with a wobbly head because the wall didn't give it proper support. The temperature seemed to be rising. I found some open space where I could walk up and down. I tried to walk as slowly as possible and tried to concentrate. Once, in Japan, a long time ago now, more than ten years back, I had been given a meditation subject by a Zen master. This subject had appeared to be a silly question at first, a question without any possible answer. I had lived with that question for more than ten years. The question had possessed me then, and it still possessed me. The Zen master had told me that the question *did* have an answer.

The question is a *koan*. A *koan* is a question from the Unknown.

What is the sound of one clapping hand?

Show me your original face, the face you had before your father and mother were born.

I am turning off the light. Where did the light go?

4

That sort of question.

What is one supposed to do with a question like that? You try to explain to the master that you don't know what he is talking about. You try to argue. You think of anything. You do anything. But the master shakes his head and insists that you give the answer, the right answer.

And then you know that you are stuck. The question has got you. It walks around with you. You sleep with it. You know that the answer is of the utmost importance. The answer is the door to the infinite, the hole in the wall which has been built around you. The wall has been there for a very long time and you really want to break it, that's what took you to the Zen master. And now, finally, there is a way out. The master knows the way out. You think that if you can get the master into such a position that he will nod at you, then the wall will crack and there will be a way out. Then you can begin to understand why you are alive.

And when, in your desperation, you ask what you are supposed to *do* in order to find the right answer, the master tells you to meditate. He explains what you have to do, how you have to sit. He shows you statues of the Buddha. He sits in the lotus position. The Zen master imitates the Buddha statue, left foot on right thigh, right foot on left thigh, back straight, head bent forward a little. He shows you how to breathe. He tells you how to become one with your *koan*. He tells you not to think, not to dream. You repeat your *koan*, over and over. You push back the evercoming thoughts. You feel a warm glow, somewhere near your navel. Is that it? What is a warm glow near your navel going to do for you?

Every now and then something pops up. You think it is the right answer and you repeat whatever it was to the master, when you visit him, early in the morning, to report your progress. He shakes his head. He always shakes his head. You become despondent and he is very kind. You are arrogant and he hits you on the head, with his hand, or with his stick. But there is no answer, just a question.

I still had the question. The Japanese master had shown me that one of the words, which made up my question, was a special word, a mantra. He had told me to forget about the answer to my question and to repeat the mantra. I had to repeat the mantra once with

5

every breath. I had learned that meditation isn't limited to the meditation hall, it can be done anywhere. For example when you are waiting for something.

And now I was waiting, for illusionary authorities who wanted to peer into my luggage and into my passport. I repeated the mantra while I paced up and down, as slowly as possible, in a tin shed at a New York airport. After a few minutes the stuffy feeling wore off and my unpleasant surroundings disappeared.

My concentration weakened and I began to think about a story which I had heard and which featured a disciple of my Japanese master. The disciple, at the time, was an American soldier, serving in the occupation army in Kyoto, just after World War II. The soldier had met the old master by accident in the street and had recognized him. How does one recognize a man one has never met? He had spoken to the master a few times.

The soldier returned to America but his own country seemed stale, empty. He wanted to return to Japan. He borrowed some money and sailed to Yokohama, on a freighter, with a fourth class ticket. The master had told him to meditate and the American did nothing else. On the freighter he sat with his legs painfully crossed. He always sat in the same place, on deck, next to a pile of rope. He gazed dead ahead and only moved when the pain became unbearable. His fellow passengers asked him what he was doing. "I am meditating," he would say.

A very fanatic disciple. Perhaps I should have sat down as well, but I kept pacing up and down, comforting myself with the thought that Zen Buddhist training has a special word for walking meditation. It is called *kinhin*. The student walks with a straight back, hands folded and pressed against the stomach. I did *kinhin* and repeated the mantra, the key to the fathomless nothing, a nothing which isn't empty.

"Don't try to get anywhere," the master had told me. "Concentrate, that's enough. If ever you manage to really concentrate you will be where you want to be."

"Will everything drop away then?" I asked, but he didn't answer.

6

But when I prepared to leave his room that morning he did say something.

"Just repeat the mantra. Let every breath hold one repetition of the mantra. Become the mantra. Forget everything else. Pay no attention to your thoughts."

"Why?"

"No reason."

So it was just because he said it.

Master. A strange word. A master and his disciples. A master and his slaves. Yes, master. No, master.

A guide. You don't have to follow a guide. But if you trust him you may as well follow.

And a disciple who doesn't trust his master leaves him.

I had left, but not for lack of faith. I had thought that I could go no further.

The American disciple stayed. When I met the American he had been with the master ten years. After I left Japan he stayed another six.

The American, whom I have called Peter, helped me when I was in Japan. When I arrived at the Kyoto monastery I had found him in the master's room, where he acted as our interpreter. I had said that I wanted to find the explanation of Life, the meaning of illusion, the clue to the mystery. They had listened to me. Even when I said that the answer to my question might be in the point where two parallel lines cut each other they hadn't laughed. When I said that there appeared to be a wall around my thinking and that the wall might be destroyed they had nodded, both at the same time.

Peter had looked after me a little, while I stayed in the monastery for a year, and after that he had taken me into his private temple where I lived for six months.

When, in the end, I left, the master hadn't shown any disappointment. "By leaving here nothing is broken," he said, "your training continues. The world is a school where the sleeping are woken up. You are now a little awake, so awake that you can never fall asleep again." Encouraging words, I had lived on them for ten years.

And my training had continued, but not in the way I had imag-

7

ined. I had thought that I would have met, in odd places, guides who would have shown me the way. Accidentally, in a strange city, in an alley, or in a marketplace. Mysterious messages would be whispered, or I might suddenly receive an anonymous note giving the address of some loft where wise men would wait for me to pass a key word. But no mystic spent any time on me. For ten years I learned, but the wise lessons were restricted to hints on how to increase capital, other people's capital. The only detached spirit I met was a very old Catholic bishop who lived in a hut in an Indian village in the South American jungle, and I was travelling and couldn't stay. We had coffee together and he smiled at me.

But whenever I was forced to stop and think, which was often, I thought of the time I had worked under the old master and re-membered the question which he had planted and which was still alive. The feeling that there might be some purpose, on this small planet suspended in limitless space, increased. The depressing gloom which had, once, forced me to ring the bell in the monastic gate, had disappeared. I now suffered sudden attacks of unexplain-able cheerfulness as if nothing which concerned me could really affect me. Meanwhile I continued to worry and was plagued by the usual assortment of human weaknesses and faults but it seemed as if a reserve had been formed, an escape, an oasis of freedom. And the promise, embodied in the old master's farewell speech, con-tinued to exist.

I wandered through several countries and busied myself with matters which grew from nothing to something and then declined to nothing again until, at last, fate took me back to Amsterdam. The causes which moved me were beyond my control. Once again I was a puppet, a doll which is activated by bits of string and metal hooks, programmed in an incomprehensible manner, and put down, now here, now there, to continue its little dance. But it had become a dance, not a depressive and painful thumping. I had begun to enjoy the game which some force, or forces, were playing with me.

The morning Peter phoned me in Amsterdam was a morning like many others. I was reading the morning's mail in the office. I rec-ognized his voice, the American accent, the slow and careful way

8

in which he expressed himself, a voice of a past which was still with me. He told me he was travelling and that he intended to stay a week in Holland. I asked him to stay in my flat. He thanked me. I asked him how he knew my telephone number. He laughed. "I had been told you live in Amsterdam, and the number is in the book." I blushed. I remembered how often he had told me not to ask, but to find out. I picked him up at the airport and he stayed two weeks.

A meeting between old friends, on the surface it seemed nothing more. He told me that the old Japanese priest was dead and that he had returned to his own country, the States. He now lived in the north, somewhere near the Canadian border, in empty country, in a forest where he had started a small farm.

I took a few days off and showed him a little of Holland. He seemed relaxed and made everyday conversation. An intelligent tourist. He seemed happy to hear that I had become a family man and that I liked my job and was doing well. An older brother, glad to hear that his younger brother has succeeded.

I showed him my office. My desk is an old-fashioned cylinder desk and on its top sits a Buddha statue. When Peter saw the Buddha he growled happily, a rumbling sound reverberating in his wide chest. The expression on his face at the moment was a mixture of craziness and solemnity. He looked like the fool of the folk tale, a man who does not act the fool but who *is* a fool. No nut or clown, but a fool who feels so deeply, and sees so far that it is an effort to return to everyday life. And when Peter, after his growl, tumbled all over my office floor I wasn't really amazed.

"Good," he said, in the way the Japanese master had said "good" on the very few occasions he had approved of what I had been trying to do at that time.

As long as Peter stayed in my apartment we got up at six and meditated for an hour. He never mentioned Buddhism or Zen. One evening I brought him his coffee and found him sitting on the floor of his room. I recognized the powerful peace which I had so often felt in Japan. I sat down next to him and reached a fairly deep concentration, much better than I had thought possible and quite beyond my own power. He left the next day and, while we were driving to the airport, I asked him whether he had finished his Zen study.

He nodded.

"Then you are a master," I said, putting it as a half-question. He didn't answer.

"Do you have any disciples?" I asked.

"Yes," he said, after some consideration. "I think you can call them disciples."

His reply shook me. In Japan I had always seen him as a fellow-disciple. An advanced disciple, of course, but no master, no authority. I could joke with him and tell him to lay off. He hadn't changed much in ten years. A little bald maybe, somewhat fatter. But a white man, with a face vaguely resembling the round innocence of Charlie Brown of the "Peanuts" strip, cannot be a Zen master. Zen masters have wrinkled faces with tufted eyebrows and slanting eyes. Their skulls are bald and gleaming and they are dressed in neat brown or grey robes, and in brocades on special days. Peter was wearing a corduroy jacket, old and shabby, and pants with bobbly knees.

But why not? I thought after a little while. Vestdijk, my favorite Dutch writer, describes Christ as a waiter with rabbit teeth and his Christ is incredibly holy and unbelievably powerful. Wisdom is not limited to Orientals. Buddhism states that all beings have the Buddha nature.

I remembered a lecture, delivered by the Japanese master in the assembly hall of the monastery. I had been there a few months and some of the monks had difficulty in accepting my presence. The master made a point of telling his disciples that *all* beings have the Buddha nature, even beings with pink faces and large feet. And when a being has the Buddha nature he can realize it, and if he does, he is a master, pink face and all.

But I was still speechless. We drove in silence and, at the very last moment, when he had his boarding pass in his hand, I asked Peter if he would accept me as his disciple and if I could come to see him in America.

Peter laughed.

"But of course."

Then he embraced me, patted me on the head and walked to the desk of the border police.

He waved from the other side of the barrier, laughed again (I was staring at him with my mouth open), and disappeared.

The loudspeakers croaked again and the crowd, its mechanism touched, stirred and started to push. The old man and I were the last to go through the checkpoint. Within an hour I was in another airplane, on my way to the far north.

This was not the same kind of journey as my journey to Japan. Then I had jumped, befuddled, into the unknown and had gone to a country which I couldn't even imagine, in spite of books and pictures. Then I moved amongst human beings who, quite apart from being of another race, seemed to be of another order. In this American plane I was sitting with people who were of my own family. Any difference was a difference in detail only. And I wasn't jumping into the unknown, I knew who would be waiting for me.

The stewardess gave me a drink and I lit a cigar. The landscape below could have been Europe. I saw huge farms, worked by machine. I recognized the cars on the highways. Some hills caught my attention. I expected temples, there had always been temples on the Japanese hills. I saw no temples. And there wouldn't be any pilgrims either, or hermits, living in caves. I wouldn't see monks, meditating at the side of the road.

When the plane landed at an in-between airport I saw glowing red neon letters. JESUS SAVES.

America is still the country of power, of success. I wouldn't be understood if I told people that I had come to "study Buddhism." Meditation is weird and enlightenment is associated with electricity. And Jesus saves. And to make quite sure the message is spelled out. The Far East is a little more subtle. If it wants to explain it hints.

When I told the Japanese immigration officer that I had come to study Buddhism he had stamped my passport and waved me on. If I had told the U.S. immigration the same story I would have been asked to wait in a little room and a senior officer would have spent some time with me and, perhaps, I might have been told to use my return ticket.

The lady in the next seat was talking to me. She wanted to know where I was going. I told her the name of the little village, close to Peter's farm. The name meant nothing to her. What was I going to do there? I wanted to visit a friend.

"You must be a foreigner," she said.

I agreed.

"What do you think of this country?"

I thought. What could I say?

"A marvellous country," I said.

She shook her head sadly. Her son had been killed in Vietnam. Her other son would have to go to the war as well. Her daughter was a hippie. "Love and peace," she said miserably. "Drugs and nightmares."

I couldn't think of a cheerful reply and offered her a Dutch sweet. She liked it and I gave her the pack.

One of my bosses had taught me that when you are selling and you have said everything and you can't think of anything else and the client is still looking at you there is only one message left. "Smile pleasantly," the boss had said. I smiled pleasantly.

"You are a dear boy," the lady said.

It had been a long journey. The lady had stopped talking and I leaned back in my seat.

You are seventeen years old. You have just passed your high school exams. You are sitting opposite your father. There is a fire burning in the grate.

"What do you really want?"

"I want to go away."

"Where is away?"

"Away" is a long journey. You know you have a question and you suspect that there must be an answer. But the answer isn't here. You try to explain.

Your father is looking at you. He warns you. He knows what your question is. He has the same question.

He tells you about a man he once knew. A businessman, rich

12

and successful. The man gave it all up. He sold his business and gave the money away. He started travelling, as a bum. He was looking for the answer.

"You know how far he got?"

You shake your head.

"Persia. The Dutch consul found him. At the side of the road. Dead. You know what he died of?"

You shake your head.

"The bubonic plague."

Your father shakes his head.

"Answer. What answer? What answer did the man find? He died."

Bubonic plague.

You take the words to bed with you that night.

Two

Until nothing is left of it

A *koan* is a question from another sphere, another dimension, and to try to solve it by using ordinary means seems a waste of time. Intelligence gets you nowhere and experience is of no help. Yet the master demands an answer. He looks at you, and keeps looking at you and insists that there is an answer.

And when you try to answer he shakes his head, sends you off, rings his little bell, points at the door, does anything to discourage you. And the next day he expects you to come and see him again and looks at you and demands an answer.

I was given the *koan* in Japan; it had taken the place of all my questions. I had tried to understand the problem, without result. Anything I said was wrong.

In the end I thought that perhaps I should *do* something. Perform an act, pull a face, never mind what. But the master refused these new answers. I couldn't find the key, nothing fitted. And now, ten years later, I still had no answer and carried the very same *koan*. A fertile egg, endlessly warmed, full of tension, but the shell wouldn't break. And yet the *koan* didn't hurt me, my fear that it would have become a throbbing infected abscess hadn't materialized. It glowed, that was all.

The master had told me that each *koan* has only one acceptable answer. He had compared the *koan* with a supreme court judgment. The judgments are public property. Anybody can look them up and what the supreme court has decided is irrefutable.

The Chinese word *koan* consists of two characters. *Ko* means public, *an* means case record.

I had found out that my particular *koan* didn't require a spoken answer. There was nothing I could say, nothing I could do. In order

14

to solve it I would have to become something, reach a certain level. And on that level I would meet the master and he would acknowledge my silence. But a master is a man of many levels.

He had told me how to reach the required level. I had to meditate and, as a second exercise, I would have to try and be conscious. To sit in meditation, to be awake while living my life.

I could never force him to acknowledge my answer. There was nothing to say, so I would have to be quiet, but there are many ways in which a man can be quiet.

And it was no use being in a hurry, perhaps that was all I had learned. I couldn't rush him. Maybe the right silence would come, maybe not. And what was I supposed to do in the meantime?

I was to do my best.

That's what the Buddha said when he died. He knew that his disciples expected a last bit of advice.

"Do your best," he said, and died.

In my impatience I had often told the Japanese master that I was doing my best, but he let it go. It wasn't true anyway. He knew exactly what I was doing, and all he wanted to hear was the right answer, or perhaps he wanted to see it, and he kept on sending me away and telling me to come back the next morning, at 4:00, or at 3:30, depending on the season. And whenever I went to see him it was dark, and cold, and deadly quiet.

And in the end I left that strange routine and returned to a world where a man makes money, marries, has a child, buys a house, a car, and life insurance.

Any cause has its effect. The journey to Japan was a cause and perhaps I wasn't surprised when, some four years later, I received a parcel from Kyoto. It had been sent seamail and it had travelled for months but finally it caught up with me. It was crumpled and dirty, a piece of cardboard. In the middle I saw the Chinese character for "emptiness," the "unborn," out of which all experience is said to come. Its pronunciation is *mu*, a basic sound, a mantra, comparable to the *om* of the Tibetans and perhaps also the *tau* of the Chinese mystics who lived long before Buddha was born.

On the left side of the character I recognized the hieroglyphs in which the master wrote his name and title and on the right he had written my own name, in the special script reserved for foreign words. No letter came with the parcel.

I had the piece of cardboard framed and it has formed the center piece of any room I have lived in since. When I looked at it I was often convinced that I would never understand its meaning, but I wasn't ever quite sure, for hadn't the master told me, again and again, that the riddle could be solved? I knew that the central character was the key to my question and that it described the universal mystery, in general and also in its most minute detail. And I remembered the master saying that the riddle would be solved *now*, always now, at the point where present and past merge, the most intriguing moment of existence.

The plane began its descent, the hilltops came closer. I saw the airport and a parking lot. I could see the cars, neatly arranged. One of the cars would be Peter's. I expected him to meet me, he knew the number of my flight. I had a map, in case he wasn't there. It was quite possible that he wouldn't be there to meet me. He might have forgotten or might expect me to find his farm on my own. I might have to hitchhike my way out.

But he was there. I saw him jumping up and down and waving and he embraced me and shouted, "Good to see you." Self-consciously I mumbled appropriate replies and remembered how careful he had been with me in Japan, during the first few days of our acquaintance, when he wasn't sure whether I was a raving madman or an innocent truth seeker.

In the car he asked me for a cigarette. He only smokes when he is nervous and then he has to ask for cigarettes for he never carries any. He talked a lot too and enquired after the people he had met in Amsterdam.

In Japan I suspected, and later reflection made the suspicion grow, that mystics have a double personality. The everyday personality, the act which is played, continues. The adept never really loses his identity or his habits. The old Japanese master liked going to the cinema to see films on Africa, he watched baseball on TV, he didn't like going to the dentist and he tried to avoid middle-aged ladies who came to ask questions. He preferred gardening to washing dishes. He liked some of the cartoons in the daily newspaper. He was a neat man, particular about the way he dressed. He enjoyed eating sour plums and drinking a special type of green tea. But all these habits, likes and dislikes were part of his personality, of his temporary appearance, they were the result of his education and his environment. He also had the master personality. He was a rare man, he knew, he knew his own face, the face which he had had long before his parents were born. He understood the why of all possible and impossible worlds, he had seen through every form, and could live without them, he knew how everything was connected. He lived in a oneness where all many-nesses are merged.

The discipline of the monastery kept me apart from the master, the old teacher lived in his own little house, detached from the main buildings. I might meet him, by accident, in the garden or in the street, which wasn't very often. But every day I met him in the *sanzen*-room where he received his disciples and where he expected me to give my answer, and in the *sanzen*-room I saw the personality of the master.

But Peter I knew fairly well. I had shared his temple for many months, I knew his moods. I knew his temper and his sentimentality. He had told me a little about his struggle with the first *koan*, and I had seen him struggle with other *koans*.

The man now at the wheel of the Volkswagen was Peter, not the master. But even so, this man was wide awake and if he had habits, a temper, moods, preferences, even fears or defects—he would know how to deal with them. And he would use them for a purpose, and the purpose would be beyond me.

I asked about the farm. I hadn't asked him much about his life in America when he came to visit me in Amsterdam. He described the farm and it seemed much bigger than I had imagined. Some forty people lived on his estate; it was a settlement, partly self-supporting, growing its own food. Cows, pigs, geese, vegetable plots. A milk factory, even a sawmill and woodworks.

The estate was his, an inheritance from his father who had bought the land for investment, many years ago when prices were still incredibly low.

"You are well out of the way," I said.

He nodded.

"Of course. The further the better. The curious can't reach us here. But one can work and meditate anywhere."

He told me about the first Japanese master who settled in the States. He had to hire a partly furnished room in a shoddy little house in a New York slum. The house was very close to a railway viaduct and when the trains passed the room shook, so much so that the master had difficulty in staying on his meditation cushions. The trains passed every few minutes. But there was no choice. The master had no money and his disciples were poor. But if there is a choice, choose. Pick the best there is.

"It is very quiet here," Peter said, "a few retired people, a few farmers and an old man living by himself, they are our only neighbors. There is only one store and if the storekeeper doesn't have what we want we have to wait till somebody goes to town. No telephone, no radio. And no bus."

"No TV?" I asked.

He shook his head.

"Do you know what is happening in the world?"

"I have a radio in the car. I sometimes listen to the news."

"Does it interest you?"

He laughed and shook me by the shoulder.

"Don't worry. I am concerned. I know about all the calamities."

"How did your disciples find you?"

The snow on the road hadn't been cleared for some time. There were some slippery spots and he had to drive carefully. He didn't answer for a little while.

"How did people find me? Let me see. A few came from New York, there is an institute over there and some training. The institute was in contact with the monastery in Japan and they must have found out that I had returned. But of those few people only one stayed. Later some of his friends came. One boy wandered out here and came to the house and never left, he had never heard of this type of training. A few came because they had been taking hallucinatory drugs and couldn't cope with their visions. At least one came with the question which took you to Japan. He wanted to know why he lived."

I watched the road and the bare trees flashing past my window. "Did you know what you wanted from the old Japanese teacher when you met him in a Kyoto street?"

Peter shook his head. "No."

I kept quiet. I didn't want to irritate him. I had asked enough already. He asked for another cigarette and I lit it for him. Conversations, he had often told me in his Kyoto temple, never clarify much. Language is misused. The only use of words is practical. Ask for a hammer so that you won't be given a pair of pliers. Ask your neighbor at table to pass the jam. If Peter wanted to explain something to me he wouldn't *tell* me what to do, he would *show* me what to do.

We had arrived. Peter drove the car into a gravel path leading up a hill and I saw a neat white-painted house, made of timber, and a few rough outbuildings and sheds.

Peter jumped from the car, walked round it and opened my door. I saw him as a silhouette against the moon, a full moon suspended above the trees.

"Welcome," Peter said and bowed. "Welcome to the Temple of Moon-spring."

This unexpected remark, and its setting, broke the dream of the journey. I now saw him as the master and I returned the bow, seriously, humbly. I was his obedient disciple, very much prepared to do my best.

Peter smiled and walked ahead, carrying my suitcase.

From the hilltop I could see the windows of seven small houses, tiny cabins with one or two rooms, partly hidden among the trees. Gnomes might have had houses like that, gnomes in an immeasurably large forest covering the entire visible landscape and even the hills shaping the horizon all around.

"Your disciples?" I asked, pointing at the huts.

"Yes. There are other houses which you can't see from here. Most of them were built by us, and we manufactured the timber ourselves in the mill. Some of the richer students got builders from outside but I don't like that, I would rather keep the money in the family."

"The family?"

Peter made a wide gesture, comprising everything around. "The family of the community. Money is scarce around here."

His two-story house looked just like all the other houses I had seen that evening coming up from the airport but once I was inside I was back in Japan. He had covered all floors with straw mats, there were scrolls hanging on the walls. I recognized them, they came from his Kyoto temple and some of them had been drawn by the old master. Only the kitchen was American with its outsize wood stove spreading a comfortable warmth and its walls hung with pots and pans. There was a refrigerator and an enormous freezer, large enough to store a sheep.

"Coffee or a cocktail?"

I asked for coffee, and grinned. I remembered my disgust when I found out in Japan that Buddhist priests drink, smoke, and have sex. My disgust had surprised me at the time for why should I have expected them to behave otherwise? Holy men are pure. But what is pure? The old master smoked a few cigarettes a day and would have a cup of *sake*, ricewine, every now and then. Peter drank, too, but not habitually. The Buddha lived such a long time ago that it is quite impossible to find out what he did and what he didn't do but Chinese legends, dating back to the early days of Chinese Buddhism, tell us about quite a few cases of alcoholic sages. Perhaps everyone should make his own rules and stick to them as long as they seem necessary. The head monk in Kyoto had once told me that everything is allowed, provided you can accept the consequences of what you do.

Peter must have read my thoughts for he told me about a young man who had arrived some years ago.

"A real holy boy. Thin and pale with long hair tied up in a bun. He was imitating the yogis and lived on a bit of rice and vegetables and some weak tea. He wouldn't even eat eggs."

I nodded. I had often wanted to be able to live that way.

"I gave him a screwdriver when he arrived," Peter said. More vodka than orange juice I thought. I knew Peter's cocktails.

"It cheered him up," Peter said.

"And now?"

"He seems all right now. Eats anything but meat. He brought his family, they look healthy too now. I have seen them drink beer with their meals."

I opened my suitcase and gave him my presents, a bottle of French cognac and a large Dutch cheese.

"Not here," Peter said. "You can take it up to the Buddha room later."

"The Buddha likes cognac?"

"I'll drink it," Peter said. "Later, when the opportunity presents itself. Perhaps I'll give you a sip."

A tabletop had been attached by hinges to the wall and he unhooked it and pulled it down and threw some cushions on the floor. We were back in Japan again. The meal he served was the same we used to eat, almost daily, in his temple in Kyoto, a thick stew of vegetables and a little meat.

"Where are the others?"

"We have a meditation week, you've arrived in the middle. Everybody is in the meditation temple, the Zendo. I'll show you the hall tomorrow; it's quite nice. We used Japanese drawings and a young architect helped us. He is very good, his job is to design backgrounds for movies, this Zendo was right up his street. If you are not too tired you can join us tomorrow, the first sitting starts at 3:30 and we sit till 6:30. After that I'll serve breakfast here."

I looked at my watch, half past eleven. It had been a long journey, my sense of time was all haywire, I wouldn't have minded spending a day in bed. 3:30 a.m. is the middle of the night.

"All right."

"You have an alarm clock?"

I had one, nice and loud. He had pity on me and suggested I should sleep late and join them in the afternoon but I was too proud to give in. Pride can be very useful at times. I had slept in the plane, I said. I wasn't at all tired. And perhaps I wasn't. Perhaps being tired is one of the many illusions we live with.

21

He showed me my room, pleasant and comfortable and lined with books. It was his own room but he didn't tell me that. That night he would sleep in a sleeping bag in the loft, a cold and draughty place. My bed was spread on the floor and he gave me the same eiderdown which I had used in Japan. I looked at the books.

"That's the old master's library. I remember them, he used to have them in his study. Chinese Zen classics. Did he give them to you?"

Peter watched me calmly. "He gave me everything. When he died I got his robes, his bowl, all his pots, anything his disciples had given him during his life. He even bequeathed me his ashes, I took them with me in an urn and buried them close by, under a tree and near a large rock. He wanted to be buried in America. Tomorrow I'll show you his grave."

"So it is true after all," I said.

"What?"

"These stories that Buddhism will go West. The East is the preparation for the West, and the West will be the preparation for the entire planet. Maitreya, the Buddha to be, will be born here."

Peter lost interest and scratched his back.

"Sure, sure," he said. "That's the history of the future. But what good is that to us now? Buddhism here, Buddhism there. What does it matter? Do something now. Have a bath. The bath should be ready. I asked one of the boys to heat the water for us."

I undressed and he gave me a bath kimono and slippers. The tub, the wooden stools, even the dented metal dishes all came from the old Kyoto temple. I washed quickly, rinsed my body and soaked in the hot water for a few minutes, and sat on the floor waiting for him. We massaged each other's backs and shoulders and had a quick cold shower. Peter said good night and I hunted for an ashtray, and made myself another cup of coffee in the kitchen.

While I smoked my last cigarette of the day I thought of the old master. His ashes were buried in the forest. His personality no longer existed, his old bones which hurt him so much during the last years of his life, were gone for ever. Nothing was left but the direct results of his lifelong labor were all around me. The line of his teaching continued, was as alive as in the days when the Buddha wandered all through India, on his bare feet.

Life is so crazy that I'll never get to the bottom of it I thought and turned over.

You are back in Japan. In an unreal green forest you are walking next to the old master. You get to a brook. The master touches your shoulder and you know that he wants you to sit down. He sits down next to you. You look up because you don't know what he wants of you. You are as aware as you can manage to be because you never know what will happen when you are in the presence of a master.

He shakes his head and points at a piece of cork floating past; it has been in a fire and half of it is black.

"That piece of cork is your personality," the master says. "At every turn, at every change of circumstances, at every conflict, defeat or victory, a piece of it crumbles off."

You look at the piece of cork. Pieces of it detach themselves and disappear. The cork is getting smaller.

"It is getting smaller," you say, nervously.

"Getting smaller all the time." The quiet voice of the master is very close. He speaks English, you have no trouble at all understanding him. "Till nothing is left of it," the master says.

You look up. You expect him to look like the roaring lion who sat opposite you so often during the days when he wanted you to solve the *koan*.

But he isn't roaring. He looks quiet and pleasant. There is only a little old man who wants to point out something to you. Nothing will remain. You will lose your name, your body, and your character. Your fear diminishes.

If it has to happen it will happen.

Nothing will remain.

And nothing you will be.

23

Three

___

The horseshoe crabs

___

It was five to three in the morning and the snow crackled under my shoes. It was well below zero and the cold made the trees creak. Peter had given me a flashlight and I was using it anxiously, I had slipped already, on a patch of ice which I had mistaken for snow and my hand was bleeding, cut on a stone. The coffee, which I had drunk too quickly, was sloshing about in my empty stomach.

It could be worse, I thought. There must be concentration camps and jails where the prisoners aren't even given coffee in the morning.

We were on the way to the Zendo, the meditation hall built by American boys from Japanese plans. We were crossing a small bridge.

"From here onwards you are on holy ground," Peter said. "Now we are very close to the Zendo, and here on the left, near that large rock the old teacher's ashes are buried. We don't talk here and we don't smoke."

I switched my flashlight off. I could see my way by the lights coming from the Zendo's windows, and now, for the first time, I saw the wooden building with its strangely shaped roof. The architect had done well with the materials at hand. The temple was quiet and powerful. There was a veranda with shelves, already filled with shoes, neatly arranged. I took mine off and wanted to go in in my socks. Peter tapped me on the shoulder. No, I thought. I won't take off my socks. But Peter did and I followed suit and walked on the cold stone tiles, very carefully, on the sides of my bare feet. Back into the silent awesome discipline of a meditation temple. A place of fear, of pain but also a place of adventure. I was older now, I should be more mature. I would suffer less, I was quite sure of that and I bowed almost cheerfully, greeting the Buddha statue at the end of the hall. When I had a chance to look at the statue I recognized it as an image of Manjusri, the Bodhisattva holding a sword, and with the sword it cuts thoughts, imagination, ego. This particular statue was very beautiful, quiet and energetic, calm and ready for anything. A bowl filled with nuts served as an offering. Very practical; nuts don't rot very quickly and don't have to be replaced all the time. Incense smoldered and the heavy smoke vibrated through the hall.

Not a bad place to spend a week in, but there was a little thought bothering me. A meditation hall, the thought told me, is perhaps a sort of kindergarten. We go there because we have told each other that we will. We have promised to spend a week in the silence of the hall. We have made rules and we have promised to obey them. In turns we walk around and supervise each other's efforts. We even hit each other, nicely of course, in a way which doesn't really hurt. But perhaps we should do this on our own. In a cabin, in a small camp right back in the forest. And there we should face ourselves, or what we think this "self" is, and destroy it, and break free. Without any discipline from outside, without a teacher who eggs us on, with tricks, with a bell, with a short stick. Who encourages and ridicules us in turn. The Buddha did it on his own.

A real holy man does this on his own, I told myself.

But you are not a holy man, I said, and sighed, and bowed to my cushions and climbed on top of them and wrenched my legs into the half lotus, right foot turned upside down and resting on the left thigh. The left foot I tucked under the right thigh. I still couldn't manage the full lotus, the ideal position, the free seat from which you can roar into space. It would come. It took Peter a long time too. I promised myself that, one day, I would sit in the full lotus. I might have to break my leg like the Zen master who had a crippled leg which wouldn't do as it was told, and before the master died he broke the crippled leg and twisted it into the right position and died in it, a few hours later. All his life he had been a slave to his leg but he died a free man.

The meditation leader rang his bell. Four strokes and four times the full sound died slowly, with tremors, ebbing away. I straightened my spine, regulated my breathing, and concentrated, for the umpteenth time, on my *koan*. In an hour or so I would face a new Zen master and present my answer to this *koan* of mine, the most prized and the most frightening possession I had ever owned. I would meet Peter in the *sanzen*-room, exactly as I had met the old master hundreds and hundreds of times in the Kyoto monastery. I felt neither excited nor worried. The attempt at concentration had become a habit. The need to force an answer had gone, long ago. I no longer wanted enlightenment. I really didn't want anything at all. I just wanted to sit, quietly, for twenty-five minutes until the jikki jitsu, the meditation leader, rang his heavy bell again. And then I would go out and stretch my legs and do a few physical exercises and come back again, and sit for another twenty-five minutes. If there weren't to be any pain it might go on forever. I felt quite peaceful and repeated the *koan* and fought the sleep which hung on my eyelids and told me to close my eyes and relax and float off. I was prepared to do my best, it was all I could do anyway. The path I had been following seemed the right one, it didn't lead anywhere perhaps but the direction seemed right and I plodded along, as the proverbial Zen ox plods through the swamp; when his feet get sucked into the mud he applies a little more strength and goes on. He can't see where he is going for the horizon is invisible. It's foggy. The ox doesn't complain, he grunts a bit, the plaintive bellowing has changed into an occasional snort.

When the jikki rang his bell I looked at my neighbors, quickly, I didn't want them to know I was looking at them. My neighbor on the right was fat, dressed in a white jersey and an enormous walrus moustache decorated his round jolly face. He was sitting in the full lotus and blew heavily through his wide nostrils, making the hairs of his moustache wave. On my other side I saw a very slight girl, or young woman. I jumped off my seat, bowed to it (cushions are always bowed to in a Zendo, they are the future, or present, point of escape), bowed again at the door, and joined the small crowd on the veranda. In Japan the monks sneaked off into corners during the short breaks and puffed at cigarettes and talked but here a pure silence ruled. Some stared out into the night, others did exercises, and massaged their legs. A very serious crowd. These were the true volunteers, the Japanese monks had been forced into the temple life by their fathers, here everyone had come by his own desire, the desire, if Buddhist philosophy is right, to break desire.

But why? Hindu philosophy has an easy explanation. Microbes are born and die and are born again. Slowly their small souls develop and a lot of microbes become one bug, a lot of bugs, eventually, become one mouse, a lot of mice, one dog, two dogs become one stupid man, the stupid man lives many lives and becomes a little cleverer. Finally he realizes his soul is caught. He wants to become free. He knows his desire to be a man, a special man, an individual, holds him back. He feels the limitations of his ego as a wall. He has the feeling that he wants to break the wall. Each life makes the desire to break desire stronger. And one life becomes the last life. He breaks his desire and becomes . . . An angel? A god? A being on another planet? A bodhisattva? The Hindus may be right. Six hundred lives or so and a man is free. Any man. He can't help it. The longer he lives, in his chain of birth and rebirth, the more evolved he becomes. The soul, the atman, becomes tired of the endless cycle. It gradually formulates the idea that liberty really exists. It feels caught. The undeveloped man doesn't feel caught. But the developed being looks for a guide, and finds a guide. Whatever you want will happen eventually. Give it time, be patient and go on wanting, and one day the guide appears, if it was a guide you were wanting. And then the trip starts, the final trip. The disciple is fearful and nervous and unhappy. He finds a lot of faults in his guide. He may want to run away, and he may, in fact, give up. But the guide will show up again. And the disciple really wants to know the way out, even if he is fearful and nervous. He can't stay where he is, he can't go back, what else can he do but try to follow the guide? And he doesn't really know what he wants to achieve because the goal, freedom, is beyond his power of conception.

Not a bad theory I thought. But I hadn't come to the Zendo to think, I had come to sit still. And concentrate, of course, concentrate on the key word. The word made my *koan*, and the *koan*. . . .

"Repeat that word till everything falls away," the old master had said. I tried and time fell away. The bell rang again, another twenty-five minutes gone. In Japan I had never wanted to believe the monks when they told me that there is no time in the Zendo. The old monks said it. The young monks knew all about time, it ticked away slowly on the jikki's cheap alarm clock. In Japan I had counted the minutes if I wasn't asleep or sunk away in some dream or other. Time was torture. But now there had been no time. The endless bubbling thoughts had been strangely absent. Miracles, after all, did exist.

The third period had no miracle. My old friend, pain, was with me again. It started as a slight tremble in my left foot and quickly became a raging fire. I moved, the pain stopped for a minute and came back again, furiously, because I had frustrated it. I moved again. The jikki spoke to me on the veranda during the interval.

"Don't shift around. You bother the other people. If you do it again I'll have to ask you to leave."

"I was in pain," I said.

"I know. We all are at times. Pain is no reason to move."

The short speech annoyed me. It was abusive, I thought. I felt alone, unable to relate to this bunch of fanatics. The young monks in Japan had moved when they were in pain and I had been able to identify with them. Here I was opposed by storm troopers, all bent to get to whatever-or-wherever-it-was exactly according to their rules and to what the master told them.

Americans make good soldiers, I thought. They win wars. And I am a European. We are fumblers, we make a mess, but sometimes our lives are interesting. If ever I get anywhere I will have got there by mistake.

But I retracked this line of thought. Don't underestimate the Americans. They saved us. If they hadn't come to Europe with their tanks and chewing gum and indifferent courage, where would I be now? In a slave camp or dead. And they had allowed me to come to this place.

But still, the jikki had insulted me with his unfeeling message. The memory of one of the Japanese monks saved me in the end. He was a conceited fellow but whenever the head monk admonished him he would smile pleasantly. I had asked him how he managed to be so patient. The other monks were easily frustrated, I had often seen them kick trees when the head monk had worked on them.

"Well," the conceited monk said, "who am I? I don't exist. I have no real identity. I am quite empty inside. A good Buddhist has to make an effort to remember his own name."

He surprised me and I couldn't think of anything to say. I knew him as a show-off. He was always telling us how clever he was at chopping wood, climbing trees, harvesting cucumbers. But then he explained it to me again.

"Who am I," the conceited monk said, "that I can be insulted?"

Sanzen came.

Guided by the jikki's eternal bell we went outside and walked to the house nearby where Peter waited, Peter the Master. *Sanzen* is the direct contact between master and disciple in formal Zen training. When this type of Buddhist training first began, in ancient China, contact between master and disciple had been very free, there were no fixed times; *sanzen*, like lightning, could strike anywhere and anytime. The master would plant his *koans* when his disciples least expected it. They might be chopping wood together, or out on a walk, and suddenly the question was there and the disciple would try to formulate an answer and the master would laugh, shake his head and suggest that the student try again, later. But when the monasteries grew and the number of disciples increased *sanzen* had to be caught in a discipline. People, whenever they live in groups, automatically make rules. Now the masters receive their disciples at set times. Peter, like the Japanese masters, continued the tradition. But his influence wasn't limited to *sanzen*-time. He might strike any time of the day. And *koans* aren't solved in *sanzen*-rooms only.

My turn came. I didn't feel tense as I ran up the stairs. Quickly I remembered what I would have to do. Three full prostrations as a greeting to the master, bow when coming into the room, bow again when leaving the room. This extreme politeness has meaning. The disciple reminds himself that he is nothing, and knows nothing.

He, from the jail of his individuality, his subjectivity, faces the ultimate, the insight of the master. Buddhism admits that the disciple, after all, *is* something. But whatever he is, he is no more than a forever changing mass of properties and habits, temporarily caught in an ever changing body of flesh. The master is very different, a being of another kind. The master also inhabits an ever changing body of flesh but he is no longer human for he has found the way to freedom and has discovered the final point of that way. The master can no longer be defined and his humanity is a mask. When the disciple prostrates his body on the floor of the *sanzen*-room he creates, for himself, a certain distance. Perhaps the daily contact with the master has led him to believe that the master is another human being, somebody he can talk and joke with. But *sanzen*, even when it is full of words and jokes, is no ordinary conversation. *Sanzen* connects the deepest part of both master and disciple, the part which is realized in the master and may be realized in the disciple. The disciple bows down in the dust, not only for the master but also for himself. *Sanzen* is, perhaps, a breakthrough. The protecting layers which cover and form the personality of the disciple are broken, peeled off, like an onion can be peeled off. And when the last layer goes and nothing remains, then. . . .

The *sanzen*-room was no novelty to me. It copied the old master's room in the Kyoto monastery. When I faced the figure opposite I knew I had not changed masters. There was no difference. The human form facing me, quietly, in deep concentration, vibrating power and peace, didn't differ from the form of the old master. At that moment I could never have said, "Hello, Peter."

I said my *koan* in Japanese, as I had been taught. When the master rang his bell I made my three farewell prostrations. Outside, on my way back to the Zendo, I realized that I had spent less than a minute in the *sanzen*-room. I had received the usual treatment. But *sanzen* doesn't consist of bows and bells. Anything can happen. In Japan I had lived through a *sanzen* which must have lasted close to half an hour. When two people meet each other in concentration the result can be staggering.

The morning session finished at 6:30. I walked back to the house.

The jikki, now appearing as a pleasant young man, in his middle or late twenties, was chopping wood and smiled at me. He introduced himself as Rupert. There was no mention of his outburst in the Zendo. The temple's demon had changed into a nice fellow.

"Are you the disciple from Holland? Peter told us about you, we vaguely knew you existed. I am glad you could come."

I offered him a French cigarette and he sniffed at the tobacco and put it behind his ear.

"You are the first Dutchman I ever met."

I looked stupid and made my moustache tremble.

"We are a mad race."

"Yes," Rupert said, "but Americans aren't quite normal either. All earth is populated with madmen."

Which was true, and I went inside.

Peter was frying eggs in the kitchen and pointed at the table where a bowl of soup was waiting for me. In Amsterdam I never have much breakfast but here, with the biting cold and the unusual strain of sitting still for hours without being allowed to fall asleep, my stomach had managed to work up an appetite. I even ate the fat fried sausages Peter put on my plate.

He sat down and grinned. I didn't say anything and ate. I knew that this was the same man who had faced me, an hour ago, in the *sanzen*-room, but I could neither understand nor accept it.

"You are welcome to sleep here tonight," Peter said, "but after that it may be better for you to live with the others. Rupert has a cabin, quite close by. I asked him to put you up, you can be of use, there's a lot of wood out there which needs chopping and stacking and he may let you cook the meals. During the day he usually works at the farm here, or at the sawmill. You can do that as well, if you like. You can organize your own daily routine, you won't stay long enough to fit in but it doesn't matter. I'll invite you both for dinner now and then and there are some people you should meet. I may visit you from time to time. Work it out for yourself."

I went on chewing and nodded. I wasn't particularly worried, Rupert didn't scare me.

"We'll have some irregular meditation the next few days and a proper *sesshin*, an organized meditation week, starting next Monday. That will change your routine again, you people will be sitting some ten hours a day."

I nodded again, I had come for that week. The first week of December is Rohatsu. December the eighth is the day that the Buddha, two thousand five hundred years ago in India, sitting under a tree in the full lotus, had found his ultimate enlightenment. All Buddhist sects celebrate the day. The Zen sect with its tough tradition has made the preceding week into an ordeal, a week of almost uninterrupted meditation. The *sesshin* is called Rohatsu which simply means "Eighth Day."

The thought of Rohatsu made me feel uncomfortable but I wasn't really frightened. I had been through a Japanese Rohatsu, with almost sixteen hours of meditation a day. No matter how tiresome or painful this American week might be, it would never beat the Japanese torture. And anyway, I had no choice. Forces were pulling and pushing me, my own forces, and I couldn't fight them. There is no choice, I was quite sure. The important events of a man's life are unavoidable. A man may think he chooses, but he only does what he has to do and later he calls, whatever it was he did, his "choice." He says he wanted to do it, but he experienced what he had to go through. A theory which is hard to prove, or disprove. Why did I go to Japan? Why had Peter suddenly appeared in Amsterdam? Why does a man stare at his own face one morning while he is shaving and why does he suddenly know that he will change the direction of his life? Why did the Buddha sit down under a tree and decide that he would not get up again until his last question was answered? Why did Bodhidharma, the first Zen master, walk from India to China to sit in meditation in a cave for nine years before his first disciple found him to start a training which, eventually, would make him the first Chinese Zen patriarch?

I helped with the washing up, chopped some wood in the garden, slept for an hour and lunched by myself in the kitchen. In the afternoon I went out for a walk. Peter's farm was close to the sea. The shore is twisted and there are many small bays and coves. Within a quarter of an hour I was walking on a rocky beach with no one around. The ice had taken strange shapes. I saw transparent bubbles, covering rocks gleaming in the sunlight. I walked on the ice and it broke under me. I admired the roots of fir trees embracing the boulders of the shore. A small squirrel abused me because I disturbed its peace. Blue birds, looking like the jays of the Dutch forests, circled around my head. They seemed tame and were probably used to being fed by Peter's disciples.

In between the rocks I found some crab shells. The crabs, I was told later, are horseshoe crabs. I picked up a shell and turned it over. Inside the legs were neatly folded and the claws still undamaged, the body itself had shrunk into a small brown ball. A long horned tail projected itself from the shell, beautifully shaped and tapering off into a sharp point.

Why did Bodhidharma come to China?
The monk points at a fir tree.
"The fir tree over there."
The master nods.
The monk might have said "the shell of the horseshoe crab."
The creation is perfect. Everything is the way it should be. There is nothing to ask, nothing to explain. There is no difference between the created and the uncreated. The mystery is with us all the time and it is no mystery.

You understand a little, very little. And while you think you understand you begin to doubt again.

And you continue walking, on a field of stones, illuminated by the afternoon's sun, or in a street choked with petrol fumes, or on a battlefield where they are trying to kill or maim you, using the most ingenious weapons which can be invented. You are a riddle and you live in riddles.

And still the answer is very close, and you know you will find it.

Four

The rhinoceros horn

That evening there was another meditation exercise, a two hour stretch. The oil heater in the hall wasn't working properly and, in order to restore our blood circulation, Rupert marched us outside for *kinhin*, meditation-while-you-walk. As our leader he had to march ahead, sounding his bell; a helper walked close to him with a flashlight. He selected a safe route, a gravel road with few obstacles.

Kinhin isn't an ordinary walk and nobody is supposed to watch where he is going. You just follow the person ahead and continue your concentration. But something went wrong and before I knew what was happening I was part of a heap of wriggling bodies getting bigger all the time as fresh weight was added to it from the back. Somebody cursed softly and a few girls giggled but we sorted ourselves out again.

I only found out later what had caused the turmoil. Two large dogs had seen us march past and had been attracted by the light and the bell. They had tried to play with Rupert but Rupert was scared of dogs and had frozen in his tracks.

It's always good sport to tease authority and it must have been months before people stopped reminding Rupert of his famous *kinhin*.

The next morning, after breakfast consisting of roast turkey-spines, fried potatoes and pickled vegetables (the latter two ingredients coming from the farm), I moved to Rupert's cabin. I knew he lived close by and started walking down the driveway in the direction

Peter had pointed out to me but Rupert called me back and pointed at the Volkswagen Peter had used to fetch me from the airport.

"Let's take my car, it's easier, we don't have to carry your luggage, it's about a quarter of an hour's walk."

"Your car?" I asked. "I thought the car was Peter's."

"It's Peter's car."

I lifted my suitcase onto the back seat where it sat next to a case full of carpenter's tools and a few tins of nails.

"How do you mean?" I asked. "Everything which is yours is Peter's?"

Rupert shrugged his shoulders. "If that's the way you want to put it it's all right by me."

I asked him to explain. The car went very slowly, ice had made the road very slippery and once or twice we nearly slithered into the bushes.

"All right," Rupert said, "I'll explain it to you. The car is mine. I earned the money which bought it and the papers are in my name. But when I arrived here the farm was short of money and Peter sold his own car, a Buick which some relative had given to him. And then he took mine. I am still allowed to use her occasionally but only if Peter has no use for her. And if she needs repairs I pay the bills."

I laughed.

"You think it's funny?" Rupert asked.

"Yes," I said.

Which wasn't altogether true. I was sorry for him as well, but I laughed because I recognized the treatment. Peter wouldn't have confiscated the car without a good reason. It might be that Rupert was very fond of his car. There were a lot of cars on the estate, Peter could have picked somebody else's car.

I also laughed because I didn't think that Rupert had expected that he would start his Buddhist training by losing his most prized possession. We take the mystical path in a most reverent mood. We are convinced that we will have beautiful experiences, we expect heaven-knows-what, such as visions and other supernatural sensations, but all we get is a pain in the legs. And when something does happen it's unpleasant.

I tried to explain my line of thinking to Rupert and he grunted his agreement.

His cabin turned out to be a wooden box on stilts, put together from logs spat out by a careless mill. An old stove with a rusty pipe gave very little heat. Rupert excused his home.

"I don't have much time. During the days I have to meditate or work, Peter is very good at finding something to do for me and I can't very well avoid him. I always intend to do something about this cabin but when I get to it I eat and go to sleep."

In the way of furniture he owned a chest of drawers and a table. The table was a piece of old board resting on four different legs.

"Driftwood," Rupert said. "I picked it all up on the beach. The money I brought went into buying the cabin; I ordered it from a factory and it came on a truck. They just dumped it here and I had to put it together myself. I wasn't very good at it then, I have learned a lot since. If there is time I'll pull it to pieces again and start all over, but there won't be time."

I found an old torn army sleeping bag on the floor near the stove.

"That's mine," Rupert said. "I collected some blankets for you, over there, in the corner."

It was quite a stack, old horse blankets. They wouldn't give much warmth but if I used all of them I might survive.

As I poked through the blankets Rupert smiled.

"I'll find you a mattress later today. You'll be all right."

I didn't feel like opening my suitcase and put it down somewhere. I didn't mind this poverty, it would be a change from the years of luxury in my apartment with all its modern conveniences. To go hungry would worry me but if Rupert didn't have enough to eat I could always go to the nearest store and buy food.

"Here," Rupert said and pressed a bucket into my hand, "go and get us some water. I can't afford a well so the water has to come from the neighbor's tap."

I went outside but saw nothing but trees. I had almost gone back to ask where the neighbor lived but remembered that Zen people do not like to answer questions. It would be better if I found out by myself. I put the bucket down and thought. I might walk back to the road and find the neighbor from there, his house would have to be connected to the road by a track or path. But the road was five minutes away. It would be cleverer to walk through the forest.

It was snowing so there were no tracks from Peter's previous water expeditions. A virginal white covered everything around me. The neighbor's house would be either on the left or on the right. I went to the right and the choice proved to be correct, I found another cabin at a quarter of a mile distance. There was nobody at home, the door wasn't locked and I went inside and found the tap.

This cabin looked very different. A home is always the projection of the inhabitant. I hadn't believed Rupert's excuse of having no time. His poverty-stricken surroundings had to be a result of something in his mind. I had been in poor people's homes in Japan and they had proved to me that it is even easier to create beauty when you have little than when you have much. Emptiness is always a good background, it sets off a flower in a simple vase, or a strangely shaped rock on a bit of shelf.

Whoever lived in the cabin of the watertap knew about this. He had built himself a fireplace and two low chairs. The chairs were made of driftwood, polished to bring out its grain and color. They were rough but graceful at the same time. The small kitchen fascinated me. Kitchen implements are usually ugly and the best thing you can do with them is hide them in a drawer but this man had welded a rack from a few pieces of iron and painted it black. The various spoons, knives and tools hung from the rack. I couldn't make out how he had managed to get their shapes into harmony but he had definitely succeeded. The antique stove was a rare find, a huge body of black castiron, perhaps a hundred years old and not just made for cooking but also for baking bread—I was told later that he had found it in an old deserted cabin in the forest.

Back at Rupert's place I started washing the dishes.

I remembered one of Peter's lessons in the Kyoto temple. I had only just moved in with him and had some difficulty in adjusting to his rhythm and way of doing things. He had been washing the dishes one afternoon and I had intended to go out somewhere. I was looking for the key to my scooter and rummaging about for it in the kitchen.

"Can I be of any help?" I asked.

Peter mumbled a word which resembled "idiot" but I thought I had misheard and asked him again, in the same cheerful manner, if I could be of any help.

"Idiot!" Peter said, very clearly this time.

The insult angered me and I pointed out that his behavior was ridiculous. I had politely offered to help him and he called me names.

"Of course I am calling you names," Peter said. "The mere fact that you are asking me if you can be of help proves that you have learned nothing at all during the long year you have been with us."

"Yes?" I asked, really angry now.

Peter had put the dish towel down and looked at me.

"Yes," he said, "you learned nothing. You know damn well you can be of help because I am doing the washing-up and you know I have a lot to do. But you don't want to help at all because you are going out somewhere. You are only asking because you want to make a good impression, to show your so-called helpfulness. If you want to be of help you would *be* of help and pick up a dish towel, which is right here on the table, we do have two dish towels, and you would start drying up."

I had left the kitchen without saying anything and in a rage and the event had never been mentioned again but I had understood that he was right.

"Good," Rupert said now, "you can finish this job and afterwards you can sweep the floor if you like and clear up generally but don't spend too much time on it because there is so much to do in the house that you could easily lose a week on it. If you are very eager you might chop wood outside, my reserve is almost gone and the little firewood I have is outside in the snow and wet through. If you can get some inside the house it will have a chance to dry and the stove might put up a better performance."

Before he left I asked how long he had been living in the cabin. He had to think before he answered.

"Oh, about a year I think. A little more maybe. I can't remember exactly. Sometimes Peter tells me to move out, usually when a family arrives. They stay here till we can build them a proper place and in the meantime I stay in Peter's loft which I prefer really. It means that I don't have to cook my own meals."

I worked until the evening's meditation. I found a little food in the house and fixed my own lunch and had an hour's sleep terminated by Rupert's alarm clock. Most of my time went to chopping wood and carrying it inside the house. I stacked a good quantity against his walls but it wouldn't last long, as the old stove gobbled the wood much faster than I had expected but the temperature didn't change much, even after I had adjusted its flue. There were draughts because of the many cracks in the walls and floor.

I wondered how I would feel if I should have to stay in the cabin for some length of time, with Rupert as the man in charge. It's easy to get on each other's nerves in a cramped space and Rupert wouldn't be the easiest fellow to get along with. But perhaps it would be quite pleasant, sharing a small cabin in a large forest. We wouldn't get bored. Meditation knows no beginning and no end. Hermits spend years at it in their mountain caves.

I thought of the short film I had seen in Japan, in a small cinema in an out-of-the-way part of Kyoto which I had found by accident.

The movie shows a ramshackle house, in the slums of a large Japanese city. The owner is no longer interested and the house has been taken over by some shady characters from the underworld. Two of its inhabitants are small-time burglars, an old couple live in an attic, the husband is an invalid and the wife goes out begging. The invalid repairs a few pots and pans but usually he lies in a corner, drunk, if possible. There is an idiot who stutters and drools and an ageing whore who is running out of clients.

Suddenly a wandering monk appears in the midst of all this misery. He wears the Buddhist robe and owns a staff, a begging bowl and a bell. The staff helps him to support his old body when he hikes through the mountains, the begging bowl provides his daily rice and with the bell he attracts attention. He has a bald head and a kind old man's face.

He is standing in the open door and asks permission to enter.

The people of the house are arguing but they allow him to come in, they have plenty of room and a wandering monk enjoys a certain respect, he may be an omen of good luck. The old man finds himself a corner and sits down. He listens to the argument. The room he is in is the living room, used by everybody, and they all claim that it is not their turn to sweep the floor that day. As soon as the monk understands what the fight is about he gets up, takes a broom, and starts sweeping.

From that moment the mood of the house changes. The inhabitants begin to help each other. The burglars bring an old blanket for the invalid. The whore begins to watch her language. The invalid says a kind word to the idiot and interferes when the burglars tease the helpless fellow. The monk is very quiet, he only talks when he has to talk. He greets politely, he wishes good morning and good night. He helps. When the old invalid dies the monk sits next to the sick man and holds his hand. When the old woman wails the monk comforts her. When the idiot cannot find his flute the monk finds it for him. He never criticizes, he never praises. When the burglars stop burglaring and get jobs as laborers at a building site the monk says nothing but he smiles when they invite him to dinner, paid for with honest money. Even the whore changes her profession, she becomes a charwoman. The film ends with a party. The people of the house celebrate New Year with a feast. After the meal there is music. The only instrument is the idiot's flute but everybody contributes. The ex-burglars clap stones together, the charwoman taps a chopstick against a bottle. Everybody sings. The song is very sensitive, delicate. The monk strikes his handbell, the sound of the bell begins to vibrate and the film ends, suddenly.

When I left the cinema I was reminded of the bookstore in Rotterdam where, as a boy, I had bought my books. Once I found a book there which interested me. It was *The Lama of the Five Wisdoms* by Lama Yongden, the disciple or teacher of Mrs. Alexandra David-Neil. At the time I wasn't impressed by eastern religions but the book cut to the bone. I told the bookseller about it and said that I had found the book "by accident." He shook his head and pointed his lips. "Nothing happens by accident," he said.

"You are not a spiritualist?" I asked suspiciously.

He cackled.

"No," he said when he had finished cackling. "But nothing happens by accident. If you buy a book here you buy something which belongs to you. The book, whatever it has to tell you, is part of you. You only take the book home and read it because you want confirmation of your own thoughts."

I hadn't understood him.

Rupert came home and was impressed by my labor.

"Let's have dinner," he said and unwrapped a parcel; it contained four turkey spines.

"Where do you get that stuff?" I asked. "Peter eats it too."

"Turkey waste from the factory," Rupert said. "We can buy it very cheaply. They have chicken backs too, but chicken is more expensive. The factory sells frozen and canned poultry but some of the stuff they can't get rid of and they sell it to the poor people around here. I buy it straight from the freezer in their warehouse."

I asked him how he got his money.

"Sometimes I get a check from home but most of it I earn. I take an occasional job in the city but usually I work right here, at the farm. Peter pays very little but his teaching is free. You get knocked about a bit when you work with him. There are all sorts of jobs here. Harvesting, looking after the cows and the pigs, a day at the sawmill or the carpenter shop, we make some small furniture here which we sell to a wholesaler. Anyway, I don't need much, I spend about five dollars a week on food."

Fifteen guilders, I thought. One reasonable dinner in an Amsterdam restaurant costs twenty-five guilders.

Rupert laughed. "Don't look so sad. Rice with turkey spine is a feast, and I have some pickles to liven it up. There is a jar of pickled cucumber somewhere, and coffee of course."

"If you lend me your car tomorrow I'll go to town and buy a week's supplies."

"Sure," Rupert said, "I'll ask Peter. You can spend your money if you have to but don't overdo it. We don't need much and too much luxury will only block the path. You came to meditate, you

41

don't need money for that, you don't even need a cushion, your blankets will serve quite well."

All right all right, I thought.

The food was delicious. I used a bent spoon and a cracked plate. I felt content and thought about my life in Amsterdam where I was spending a lot of time and energy on marketing a product the world could do without. And in exchange I was earning an excellent wage which bought me all the food and clothing and extras my family and I could possibly use. I could eat from a very special plate, created for me by a master potter, and use a silver spoon.

A waste of time and energy perhaps. But what else was there? Should I come here and live in a log cabin? Who would pay the bill if my wife were to be ill again, or my child? I shook the thought off. I wouldn't come and live here. I would stick to my own environment and Rupert could stick to his. I would come here if I was forced to and I couldn't see anything forcing me yet.

While I thought my eyes wandered through the room and I saw a strangely bent piece of driftwood which Rupert had nailed to his wall. A decoration? I pointed at it and asked.

"Why did you put that up? Were you trying to beautify the cabin?"

Rupert looked. "Ah," he said. "I found it. What does it make you think of?"

I thought carefully, Rupert didn't go in for chitchat. Everything he said had some meaning.

"A rhinoceros horn?"

Rupert nodded. "Exactly. It couldn't be anything else. I found it on the beach, it must have been there for years, it is very nicely polished."

I tried to work out why Rupert would be fascinated by a rhino's horn. Everything which I knew about rhinos passed through my mind, it wasn't much.

There would have to be some connection. With Buddhism most probably, the only subject which was of real interest to my host. Japanese Buddhism. There are no rhinos in Japan. Perhaps in the Kyoto zoo, and suddenly I had the answer.

"Hakuin," I said.

Rupert smiled.

Hakuin was the Japanese Zen master who revived the Zen sect in his country. In China Zen had almost disappeared and in Japan the training was ebbing away. The monks in the Zen monasteries were taking it easy, reading and gardening but they meditated as little as possible and the teachers were slack, forgetting about the *koans* or passing their disciples on the merest hint of understanding and insight. Hakuin was dissatisfied and wandered around, looking for answers which would explode his questions. His training was a haphazard affair, whenever he thought that he had found something he would meet a hermit or a pilgrim who either ignored his insight or made him ridiculous. Eventually he started meditating in out of the way places by himself and real insight began to come and later, when his insight was acknowledged by one of the rare real masters of that time, he began to teach.

During one of his early wanderings through Japan he saw a rhinoceros. It was part of a travelling circus and Hakuin was impressed by the power and size of the extraordinary animal.

You think you understand something.

You are sure you finally know a little.

You think you have opened the door.

But all you find behind the door is the rhinoceros. . . . The rhinoceros of doubt stands before you, and looks at you with his little eyes, and shakes his huge head.

How often have I met the rhinoceros?

Again and again. Again the powerful doubt, which stands there confronts you with his mighty size, and points his double horn straight at your forehead.

The horn which hangs on this wall.

Five

The falcon

I wanted to help Rupert with the washing-up but he interfered after I had filled a dish with hot water.

"Let it go. I'll do it. I've got the car today and I am driving to the meditation hall. I would suggest that you go there on foot. Walking to the Zendo is part of the exercise. It's a lovely night anyway, the moon will light your path and the trees are covered with fresh snow. You won't see anything if you have to peer through the blurred car windows."

While I put on my sheepskin-lined overcoat I complimented myself on my change. Rupert treated me in about the same way Peter had treated me in Japan. But then I had usually protested, often quite elaborately, with long arguments based on logic, with gestures, with facial expressions. At that time I refused to be fussed over, and I considered my freedom, my individual way of doing things, as holy ground, out of bounds to outsiders. I was prepared to make an attempt at following the training, but only along general lines, any detail would have to be my own choice.

It seems that the training which master and "advanced" disciples give to the beginner is largely based on creating real consciousness. Everyone who walks this planet lives along a routine. As soon as we are faced by new circumstances we look for the road of least resistance. We drive to work via the shortest route. We arrange our work in such a manner that we can achieve as much as possible with as little strain as possible. We invent, often without being aware of it, a great many defense tactics. And once the routine is formed we follow the dotted line with our eyes closed. During the interval between getting out of and into our beds we avoid all

44

obstacles and, in the event we can't avoid them, we build a bridge or cut ourselves a path through the jungle.

And should anyone appear who tells us that it must be done *otherwise* we lose our tempers and try to get rid of him.

But the moments of change are of importance. At those moments we are forced to wake up and look around. And only when we are awake do we see something, and there is much to be seen. We live in a miraculous world. I saw it when I left the cabin. Rupert's dishwashing noises faded away as I walked down the track. The trees were cut out of the night sky as living skeletons. The thin twigs forming their extreme border moved slightly in the weak wind.

The first time that I suspected the miraculous nature of life also had to do with trees. I had forced my body into the open luggage space of an old-fashioned MG sportscar and was twisted in such a way that I was practically lying on my back and could see nothing but the sky and the treetops of the forest we were driving through. This sudden change in my method of observation knocked something loose and it seemed as if I had, very abruptly, been released from prison. A similar experience, of the same order but less powerful, now occurred on a forest track in the United States.

When I got to the highway I noticed that I was not alone. Shadows crackled their way through the snow all around. There was no need to exchange greetings. These were Peter's disciples who had just left their cabins and camps and were tramping towards the Zendo for their evening meditation. I regulated my speed so that I could walk by myself, nobody required my immediate company and I could do without theirs. This shared separation gave us companionship on another level. I didn't know their names but we were going to the same place with the same intention.

What intention? And there you are again. I used to have all sorts of replies. I wanted to know why I was alive. The purpose of existence. The insight of the Buddha. The point without questions. The destruction of ego. The one-ness with everything. Or, but that had been stressing it a bit, the meeting with God. Now I no longer knew my own intention.

I was walking to a meditation hall, a wooden temple heated with an oil burner, with the idea of spending three hours in there, sitting still with or without a pain in my legs. Somewhere in that period of time I would spend a few minutes in a small room in a nearby house. I would face a man dressed in a black robe. Candles would burn, and incense. I would try to answer a question which dealt with a subject which, by its very nature, would be well outside my scope of imagination.

And the others, walking ahead and behind me through the snow, moved in the same situation. Perhaps some of them might have found an answer to the first question, but that answer would have led them to other questions which would take them, slowly and most probably by degrees, into a weird world. A world which cannot be described but only hinted at, and which can only be discussed, if there would ever be any point in discussing it, with someone who has walked the same, or a very similar, road.

I felt the *koan* in my belly. It glowed. I repeated it a few times. The glowing became somewhat more noticeable.

I heard a car and made way. The green VW passed me slowly. I saw the outline of Rupert's head and shoulders behind the wheel. How had *he* come here? What motivated a Ph.D. psychologist to live in a draughty wooden box on stilts in a forgotten cold corner of his vast country? Peter had told me that Rupert had been well off once, living in a luxury apartment in a large city and earning a high salary. Had our consumption-society disgusted him so much that he now preferred to tear a bit of meat off a turkey spine and eat it with a piece of old bread? Or was it merely a matter of *karma*, the relentless forceful logic of causes and events, which had simply taken him by the scruff of his neck and dumped him here, in an apparent hopeless conflict with a power which attacked from a level he himself could not reach? I recognized the small female and the fat fellow, trudging through the snow nearby. Peculiar people, all of them. Crazy people, very crazy.

The fat fellow reminded me of another, one of my Amsterdam acquaintances, a man I sometimes do business with. I hadn't seen him for some time and suddenly ran across him in the street. We met near a cafe and he invited me in for a cup of coffee. I was busy and refused but he put a heavy hand on my shoulder and looked at me strangely, smiling a little, sadly, the sadness stressed by his heavy dropping cheeks and the trembling of his many underchins.

In the cafe I asked him how he was.

"Fine," he said. "I have had a heart attack."

This conflicting statement made me stop and my head, instead of being filled by a host of nervous and short-lived thoughts, became empty. I looked at him, and noticed what I saw.

"Heart attack?" I asked. "Serious? You mean you nearly died?"

"Yes," my friend said and offered me a cigar. "Nearly dead, and I may have another attack soon, and that one will kill me I suppose."

"But you are still young," I said. I knew he couldn't be more than forty-five years old at the utmost.

He nodded. "I am still young. But I have always lived the wrong way. I eat too much and drink too much and I have always worked too much."

There was no point in contradicting him. I have used him as an example, when talking to others, an example of how one should not live. In business it is easy to overdo things. There seems to be no limit to what we can sell, and once the merchandise is sold it has to be bought, or manufactured. There is no peace at all. You phone five people, you write ten letters, and you jump into a car and twist your way through the city and race for hours on the highways. And in between you eat, and drink, and smoke.

"And one day," my fat friend said, "I was driving through one of the suburbs and felt something was wrong. I had no idea what was wrong but whatever it was, it was very wrong. I was on my way to an important and urgent appointment but the feeling of misery which cramped my entire body was so tremendous that I parked the car and got out. I happened to be near a park and I had some sandwiches on the seat next to me. I took the sandwiches and fed them to the ducks in the park. It must have been the first time in twenty years that I had fed the ducks. They came waddling and flying from all directions and I fed the last and the silliest first. But the feeling continued. When they had finished my sandwiches I left them and sat in my car again."

I sucked at my cigar and studied my friend. His forehead was wet with sweat. While he talked he stirred his coffee slowly. I touched his hand and he stopped.

"I couldn't breathe. I was suffocated and I was also paralyzed. Only my left arm still functioned. I managed to open the window and get my arm out. I made it flap up and down. Cars passed. Nobody paid any attention. A chap with a beard driving a cheap little French car waved, he probably thought I greeted him."

"Amusing," I said, "a jolly story."

"The story of a man who is sentenced to the death penalty," my friend said.

"I have also been sentenced to the death penalty," I said, "and so has everybody else."

"I know," my friend said, "maybe that's why I am telling you this."

I drank my coffee and we were quiet for a little while.

"And then somebody stopped. A nice gentleman in an expensive car. He had driven past me at first but turned at the traffic lights and came back. He asked me what was wrong but I could hardly talk."

"Heart," I said and, "hospital."

"A nice gentleman in an expensive car," I said. "Strange. It would have been more likely that the chap with the beard might have stopped."

"Never underestimate nice gentlemen. He left his car and helped me move over to the passenger seat and drove me to the hospital. They kept me for six weeks, in a room with grey walls. There was nothing I could do in there, I didn't even look at the newspaper for the first few weeks."

"And now?" I asked. "Are you working again?"

My friend made his heavy cheeks tremble and began to laugh.
"I don't do much anymore but I sell as much as ever. But the battle is lost. I can't change my bad habits, they have been with me for too long. If I don't work as much as I used to it's because I have less energy. And perhaps I have seen through the foolishness of

activity. It's so easy to worry about business and when you worry you lose the right direction and you run in circles and waste time on the unnecessary. I know what I can sell where, and if I manage to get there at the right moment I usually get the order. I don't worry about losing anymore, because I am going to lose it all anyway."

I sucked desperately on my cigar. I thought of the Zen master who said that his first insight-experience was recognition of the others. Anyone he met had his own face. There was no difference between the waiter who was serving our table, my fat friend and myself. There is only one human being. The story, as told by my fat friend, was my story, and the waiter's story.

"Go on," I said.

"Right. Well, I live differently now, It's another life. I no longer look for the shortest route from A to B. I keep a loaf of bread in the car and I feed ducks and seagulls. Sometimes they aren't interested but I don't mind. I just leave the bread for them, I break it up in small pieces and leave it at the waterside. I go for walks near the river. And I am very nice to my wife. She is a short-tempered woman and I have always held it against her; now I no longer care."

"She is still short-tempered?"

"Yes. She worries about my death I think. And I still eat too much, of course, she gets very upset about it. But I don't answer back. I make her a cup of tea in the morning, she always wanted me to but I never had the time."

He looked at me and cleared his throat.

"I say," my friend said. "You are a Buddhist of sorts, aren't you? Do you know what will happen to me when I die? Do you people believe in a heaven and a hell and purgatory and so on?"

I had expected the question.

"I don't know if I am a Buddhist," I said.

My friend smiled pleasantly.

"Sure," he said. "But you must have some idea about life after death. Tell me."

"You have heard about the *Tibetan Book of the Dead?*" I asked.

He became very thoughtful. "Yes. I have heard about it. Some sort of dream sphere where your thoughts take form. But it isn't real as far as I could understand."

"Why wouldn't it be real? Is what you see now, here in this car, real? Am I real?"

My friend nodded emphatically. "Of course. You are real. I recognize you. I know your name and what you do for a living and who you are married to and the make of the car you drive."

"Perhaps I got divorced and perhaps I sold my car."

He nodded.

"Your car was getting old," he said, "but you mustn't get divorced. You have a very nice wife."

"It's just an example," I said.

His cheeks began to tremble again.

"All right, all right. But where am I going to? And how long will I stay over there? And am I coming back? If I have to come back the earth will be even more polluted and there will be even more people and we will all live above and under each other in small concrete cubicles and we'll probably feed on imitation meat manufactured by automatic machines and packed in cartons. It will be impossible to travel. I don't want to come back to such a world. And I don't really want to leave this one. Hell will be unpleasant and heaven may be a bore."

"Are you bored now?"

"No," he said. "On the contrary. I find life very interesting, more now than ever before. I saw a falcon this morning. I was driving on one of the state highways and I saw an interesting name on a traffic sign. Some little village I had never been to. I turned off the highway and the village was old, very picturesque. I sat on a low brick wall and a falcon came. It stopped, flying very close by and I saw its tailfeathers, looking like a small Japanese fan, perfectly made."

"But if you find this life interesting—why would the next life be boring then? Perhaps there'll be falcons over there as well. Perhaps they'll allow you to be a falcon yourself, after all, it will be a world of dreams. If you can be a falcon you can stand still in the sky and your tailfeathers will be stiff and spread out."

He paid and got up.

"Yes," he said, "I see. You don't know either. But thanks anyway. I wouldn't mind being a falcon for a while, this heavy body is annoying at times."

I looked at the back of the fat fellow walking ahead of me. This man was younger than my friend in Amsterdam and if he had bad habits he might still be able to change them. Even if he didn't want to change, the training here would be of help.

In the Zendo I bowed to the Buddha statue on the altar. I bowed to my cushion, turned round and bowed again. That way I expressed respect for the man whose teaching had started this religion, to the seat where "I would gain my insight" and to all beings around me. Nonsense, I thought. The Buddha I have never met, the cushions are too hard and uncomfortable and I am not, at least not at this particular moment, interested in the beings surrounding me. And why bow anyway? The Japanese bow, the gesture is automatic to them, but we greet differently. I climbed on my cushion, twisted my legs into their proper positions and stretched my back. My belly pressed itself out and the *koan* began to glow again. Rupert, at the far end of the temple, well outside my view, clapped his pieces of wood together and began to ring his bell. Four times the heavy metal sound expanded and ebbed away. The meditation had started. I repeated my *koan*, as quietly and as slowly as possible. The thoughts came, as always, and flitted about in their undisciplined and silly ways. But I sat well and the *koan* gradually became the center of my concentration. Three periods of twenty-five minutes each passed. The fourth period started. Rupert shouted *"Sanzen"* and the first group of disciples left the Zendo. I was part of it, being close to the door. We walked in line, quietly. I slipped on a piece of ice and fell. The fat fellow stopped and stood next to me. I got up and shook my head, I was all right. He began to walk again.

We entered the house and knelt in the sitting room. Upstairs, in the *sanzen*-room, the small handbell of the master called the first disciple. My turn came.

The falcon

You kneel down.

The master looks at you.

You state your *koan*.

The master keeps looking at you. The silence becomes tangible, you can hear the silence.

Tension mounts, very quickly.

And then, for the first time, you are very close to him. There is no distance.

You say nothing, the master asks nothing. Who or what you are is paper-thin. The veil is torn.

The master smiles.

The silence continues and then he gives you the next *koan*.

You have a new question and you are in another world.

For a very short moment.

Later you will know that you have been there.

Six

The crack of the door

The Kyoto monastery attracted many foreign visitors. Some came to be awed by the architecture of the buildings, the splendor of the gardens, and the austerity and discipline of the monks. Some wanted to see the master who, they were sure, could solve all their problems by merely looking at them. Others were prepared to stay a few weeks to look around, to discuss, to wonder. And some were prepared to stay longer and join the meditation. One, an old English lady who belonged to the last category, persistently sought me out and tried to gain whatever it might be she wanted to gain through my intermediary. She would wait for me outside the gate at the time I had to go to my Japanese lesson and I found it difficult to avoid her. She would wait near my scooter and I needed the scooter to go to town. She would also join me when I went for a walk in the neighborhood and during one of these walks we passed a temple where some priests were chanting *sutras*, the preachings of the Buddha. The priests sang in choir, accompanying themselves on gongs and drums and their music was impressive. The old lady started telling me about vibrations. Apparently clairvoyant people can *see* the vibrations of sound and she described to me how great clouds of color were being formed by the chanting of the priests and how lovely these colors were.

She irritated me and, after having tried to be polite to her for weeks, I finally lost my temper. I didn't say much and when I had said it, abruptly left and refused any further contact with her.

I didn't know that an English speaking Japanese priest, who happened to be passing at that moment, had overheard me and had reported my exclamation to Peter and the master. Both were very amused with me and their amusement came close to approval.

What I had said, I was told later, was: "SHIT, Madam, leave me alone with your colors, all I want is enlightenment."

And by "enlightenment" I meant that I wanted to solve my *koan*, and reach the magic sphere at the other side of the wall.

And now the moment had come and I left the master's rooms with tears in my eyes, but as soon as I started walking back to the Zendo my brain began to work and a small voice spoke. "You passed your exam."

Another little voice, a malicious one this time, asked: "Did you have Satori?"

Because, according to the Zen books I had read and the stories I had heard solving a *koan* is accompanied by *satori*, enlightenment. What this may be the books and stories do not say for the experience cannot be described. But the reader, or listener, will have some idea of what this experience could possibly be. I had always thought that *satori* would somehow be connected with light, everything would suddenly be very clear.

I had not, however, noticed any light.

The experience hadn't been spatial either. I had imagined that *satori* might mean "entering the fourth dimension." But everything around me was three-dimensional.

My hearing hadn't improved either.

So, what *had* happened?

I had to admit that nothing had changed very much. Perhaps I might now have a more intense realization of relativity, a better idea of the non-importance of what concerned me. But that was nothing new. Detachment is caused by a slow process, and the results of this process, if any, are gradual. It was quite possible that I was merely imagining my improved sense of detachment. If I were suddenly to be subjected to torture I would, most probably, scream as loudly as I would have done before the experience.

"You shouldn't exaggerate," I told myself.

So nothing had happened? I had merely had a little conversation with a man who is addressed as "master" by his disciples?

That's what it was. I had taken part in a little conversation. Somebody had asked me a question and I had answered the question, it was true that I hadn't actually said anything, but silence is also an answer.

And now I had a new question.

And should I be glad now? When I had passed my school examinations I had been glad too. But they hadn't changed me. People who didn't know me couldn't have noticed that I had passed an examination.

But had I changed now?

In England there is a Buddhist sect guided by a master, a man who was a monk, for twenty years, in India or Ceylon, and who is said to have the complete insight of the Buddha. He gives bibs to his disciples, small pieces of cloth which they can hang around their necks and which are kept in place by a cord. The beginners have mere pieces of cloth but as they proceed along the way they are permitted to embroider their cloths. The embroidering is done with gold thread. The more insight, the more gold thread. Very advanced disciples have cloths which are thick with gold thread.

But I didn't have a bib. Nobody could see that I had learned something.

Except Rupert. At the end of the meditation I met him, he was waiting for me under a tree. I wanted to pass him in silence as he had told me that the walk from and to the Zendo are part of the meditation but he greeted me and walked next to me. He had left his car at Peter's house. It was snowing and I had put up the collar of my heavy coat; he couldn't see my face. We walked with difficulty, there was a gale blowing and we had to struggle against the force of the wind.

"Something happened," he said.

I said nothing. He put his arm around me for a moment.

"Something happened," I said.

That evening, sitting on the stack of old horse blankets in Rupert's cabin, and drinking very hot coffee from a dented mug, I tried to think. Rupert, partly hidden by his sleeping bag, had draped himself around the stove in a crescent. He was scribbling in a notebook. I also kept a notebook. I had written down some impressions, each one carefully dated.

Today's note was "solved *koan*."

I had intended to write more but I didn't know what. I should be an advanced disciple now but the fact hardly interested me. I wanted to know what exactly had happened to me. To "me," the "me" which Buddhism does not acknowledge. According to the *dharma*, the Buddhist teaching, there is no self. Instead of a "self" there is a constantly changing combination of properties, housed in a constantly changing body. But this constantly changing combination of physical and spiritual characteristics *does* exist and we may, without any criticism from the teaching, safely assume that this combination is "us" or "me." The assumption is practical and makes it possible to discuss a man called John Jones. John Jones is considerably shorter than the "constantly changing combination etc. which is, temporarily, named John Jones."

Following this way of reasoning I could safely state that "I" was here, sitting on a stack of horse blankets drinking coffee, and that, during the course of that evening, something had happened to "me."

Perhaps it would be better to start at the negative side. Did I have fewer worries now than I had, for instance, yesterday? I tried to imagine what sort of worries I could have. I couldn't think of any. After some effort I remembered that I didn't know where my keys could be, I had been looking for them on the plane, perhaps I had dropped them somewhere. But I could buy duplicates, all I had to do was borrow my wife's keys the minute I came home.

I might, if I really wanted to, worry about my family and the company which employed me, and about politics and the state of the world. But there wouldn't be much point in the activity. There was nothing I could do about humanity's problems, certainly not here, in this draughty cabin in a nameless part of America. Did this mean that I had finished with fear?

No. I still had fears, even if I couldn't name them they would be there nevertheless. Fear of death perhaps, even though death still seemed a long way off. Fear of the monsters I had seen during meditation.

It had happened that particular night. I saw the head of a small dog, a head with a lot of hair. At first the head seemed quite harmless, friendly even, but the eyes were cold and without expression. I tried to get back to my concentration but the head kept on staring at me. It became a composite of other pictures which grew from and in the dog's skin. The more I looked the more I saw. There were a lot of heads and some of them belonged to real horrors. Bats with fangs, leering demons, skeletons, old wrinkled women with running sores. Still, I hadn't been really frightened, I had been visted by these visions before and I knew that, provided I didn't try to look away, the pictures would fade and eventually disappear. And perhaps the exhibition had amused me. A famous alcoholic has claimed that the mice, lizards and chameleons which he saw during delirium tremens hadn't frightened him at all. The animals could perform quite cleverly and he enjoyed watching them.

In Japan I had been told a story about a small girl. The girl had died and found herself in the in-between sphere of death and re-birth, the "Bardo" as the Tibetans call it. She saw monsters. The monsters were her own projections, living forms representing her fears and mistakes, and with a real, albeit temporary, identity. Like any apparition, they would fade away after a while. But the girl, who felt lonely, and was a playful little thing, knowing nothing of the philosophy of her faith, merely recognized parts of these horrors as familiar images. They reminded her of the demons who protect Buddhist temples, large statues which adorn the gates of the religious buildings of Kyoto. She went straight up to them, put out her hand, and the monsters had to obey the rule that there is no defense against kindness, and obediently played with her.

"What am I frightened of?" I thought, listening to Rupert's snoring. He had switched off the light after having wished me a good night. Only the ego can be frightened, only the ego can lose property, be insulted, be hurt, feel pain. The ego, being a flimsy construction and being bound up in time and space, will have to fall apart. The ego, in fact, continuously falls apart and has to be reinforced by vanity, greed, jealousy and evil.

"Nothing to worry about," I thought. Gradually the desire for ultimate escape to freedom, aided by training, will break the forces of ignorance. The process may take a couple of million years and a countless number of lives, on any conceivable and inconceivable level. It's all a matter of time, a lot of time.

But had there been any change? A difference in "me" before and after the treatment?

I couldn't find any difference.

But still, according to the definitions which I had found in the literature of Zen, I should be enlightened by now. A holy man of sorts. A beginner on the right and real path who has reached the end of stage I, or stage I(a). I put the mug down, lit a cigarette and got underneath the blankets. I kept my clothes on, it was very cold in the cabin. The draughts reached right into my refuge and I found my coat and lined the wall behind me with it. The coat was so thick that it stood up on its own.

I had to laugh, this was the moment which, while in Japan, I had tried to reach by any means I could think of. And now that the moment had come I wasn't even excited. And still there wasn't the slightest trace of disappointment, I didn't feel as if I had gone to a lot of trouble for nothing. I didn't doubt Peter's qualities as a master, and I didn't doubt my own status as a disciple.

But of one thing I was sure. I hadn't broken the chain of reincarnation. According to Buddhism, and, I believe, several other methods or religions, a man will be born, and a man will die, time and time again, until the moment where he reaches freedom. The possibility of breaking free always exists. All he has to do is reach pure concentration on escape. The moment he manages to stop thinking of his imitation "I," the moment he acknowledges that this "I" has no substance at all, he is free, definitely and altogether free, and he will never be born again. He may choose to die at the moment of liberation or he may choose to continue his life until death comes naturally and takes his body, but from that moment of freedom he will live as an actor, carrying masks, playing roles of heroes and anti-heroes. No further *karma* is formed, there is no cause and effect, whatever he does is without consequence. He can, like the fat Buddha with the bulging belly, the silly smile, and the bald head who presides over most Chinese restaurants in Amsterdam, sit at the side of the road and laugh his head off. If, of course, he wants to.

I woke up from a nightmare. I had been dreaming that I was in the old warehouse in the inner city of Amsterdam where the company I work for does its business. My partners had decided that we would start dealing in secondhand furniture, and the street was filled with trucks full of old and broken chairs, tables and cupboards. We were hoisting the rubbish up by hand and the warehouse was rapidly being filled, suffocating me. There was no space left to walk about in. I tried to protest but had no voice. But the nightmare ended well. While I looked desperately about I remembered that an unpleasant situation does not have to be accepted. At that very moment a gale started outside. The warehouse's doors were blown open by the furious wind and all the trash was sucked out. Suddenly I found myself in a large open space, decorated by the seventeenth century beams supporting its ceiling.

I woke up and looked around. I still felt a little suffocated. The alarm clock went off and Rupert peeled himself out of his sleeping bag.

"Very stuffy here," he said, "the stove must have been burning badly again. I'll open the door."

"Did you have a dream too?" I asked.

"Yes," Rupert said, "a nauseating dream but I can't remember now what it was about."

I washed, using very little water for I didn't feel up to the walk to the neighbor's house. Then we had a long leisurely breakfast. We made toast using a rusty pop-up toaster with a faulty mechanism. Every time the toast was ready I had to hit the machine while Rupert held on to it. I ate sausages with cranberry jelly, a strange combination which tasted surprisingly good. I had made a pot of English tea while Rupert hovered around suspiciously. The stove was burning well. A general feeling of comfort prevailed.

It was late: 6 a.m. Normally we should have been up by 2:30

but this was a day off, the day before the start of Rohatsu, the dreaded week.

Peter came in. He stamped his boots, they were covered with snow, and rubbed his red hands.

"You are up and about already? I thought you would sleep until eleven today and fully expected you both to be rotting in bed."

Rupert looked upset and Peter laughed.

"Never mind," he said, "I know how energetic you are. I am sure you have a full program for today, although I wouldn't know what could possibly be in it. It seems your guest has done most of the work around here. There is so much wood stacked around that you'll be all right for the rest of the winter."

Rupert filled his mouth with toast and jelly and made an inviting gesture towards the table. I poured an extra cup of tea and dished some sausages onto a plate.

"You aren't very nice," I said, "you haven't changed much."

Peter shook his head and looked at me. He must have remembered our Japanese days and the conflicts of that time for he began to laugh again.

I told him about my nightmare. He listened attentively and when I got to the gale which emptied out the warehouse he jumped up.

"That's it," he shouted. "Excellent. That's the way it goes."

Rupert gave me an admiring glance.

"Good dream," Rupert said. "I never have dreams like that. My nightmares always end badly, the enemy catches me and tears me apart."

When Peter had finished his breakfast he changed his face. While he ate and talked he had been a pleasant friend, now he became the boss, the organizer. I studied the strong lines of his face, the wide jaw, the blue, somewhat bulging eyes, set far apart. An extraordinary man, a man in complete control of his own behavior, who can act whatever role he has in mind and who can, for as long as he likes, refuse any other part.

Rupert was sent off, he was told to report at the sawmill. A day off never meant that the disciples could do what they wanted to do. A day off meant a day without meditation, no bells, no clappers. But the exercise never stopped, it went on, in another way.

"I've got something for you as well," he said, looking me in the eyes. "Rupert said yesterday that you wanted to do some shopping in town. You can use the car, I've got her with me. You can drop me off and go to town by yourself. I want you to run a few errands for me. There's an axe without a handle on the backseat and I need some new circular saws for the mill. And you can deliver this parcel for me, the address is on it."

Rupert came back to fetch his gloves and glanced at the parcel. "Robert?" he asked Peter. "I thought you said that you had finished with him."

Peter raised his voice. "You think too much," he said, "you are like the detective who's got a theory. It is a nice theory and he really believes in it. And then he gets another fact and it won't fit. So what does he do? Does he throw his theory away?"

Rupert looked amazed. The detective was new to him.

"He does not," Peter said. "He twists the fact until it fits his theory."

"Yes," Rupert said and left. I had expected him to slam the door but he didn't. The door closed very meekly. Peter smiled.

In the car I asked my big question. I didn't know where Peter wanted to get off so I asked my question right away. I risked a rebuff but a disciple who won't take a chance may miss an opportunity.

"Peter," I said, "please help me out. Yesterday I solved my *koan*, you smiled at my answer and gave me a new *koan*. *Sanzen* is no bullshit. Something tremendous must have happened."

I hesitated. I didn't want to look at him. I felt he was waiting. "But I didn't have any real experience. When I read the old Zen stories there was also always some mention of '*satori*.' Hakuin, the greatest master of them all, claims to have had sixteen great '*satoris*' and a lot of little ones as well."

Peter didn't answer and, with some difficulty, I turned my head so that I could see him.

"Forget it," Peter said. "Allow Hakuin a hundred *satoris*, or two hundred if he wants them."

The message sank in after a while.

"O.K.," I said, "but where am I now? I've got to be somewhere. But where?"

"You've got your finger in the crack of the door and this is where I want to get off. Drop me near that little camp over there. When you get back you can leave the car at my house. Don't come in, just leave the key in the ignition. There's never been a car stolen here yet."

My finger in the crack of the door. So the door was open. I only had to push it. An open door is better than a wall without any visible opening. But what would I find at the other side of the wall? A bewitched landscape? Or reality? A fundamentally different type of experience?

And had I been in that world, the moment when I solved the *koan*? It seemed I had been there. But I wasn't there now. I was an ordinary man in an ordinary car on my way to an ordinary town. Or did I imagine that everything was so ordinary?

The last thought fascinated me. This could very well be the answer. Not a new answer, however, I had always *imagined* that I lived in an ordinary world. And what exactly *is* ordinary?

I saw trees at each side of the road. A seagull floated in the sky. A large black car overtook me.

Isn't it true that the miracle manifests itself at every moment? Aren't you, the shadow performing its act, the Buddha himself?

Seven

The harelip

If you do something do it well.
My father had often said, and the teachers at school.
The Zen-masters say it, and their head monks:
When you walk, walk, and don't totter.
When you sit, sit, and don't wobble.
Watch it.

I remembered Peter telling me to "watch it" once. I was living at his temple at the time. There was no meditation at the main monastery that night and I had been on my way out when he stopped me near the gate where he was trying to repair something on his scooter.

"Hey," he called and I walked over to him thinking that he wanted me to hold a tool.

"You are going out?"

"Yes. I told you this afternoon. I have been invited to dinner by so-and-so and his wife."

"Watch it!" he said and turned back to the scooter.

He had amused me that time for so-and-so and his wife were nice steady elderly Japanese who would give me a formal dinner, some quiet conversation and tea and cookies. They didn't even drink *sake*, there wasn't the slightest chance that anything would happen. I laughed on my way to the dinner. A few days before I had also gone out, he had also been working on his scooter at the time, I had also walked past him and he hadn't said anything except a pleasant greeting. But that night I had gone out with some young wild Americans and I hadn't returned till the early hours. And Peter had known exactly what I was up to.

But I stopped laughing when I recalled that Peter never said anything without a purpose. If he said "watch it" he meant "watch it" and all that evening I tried to watch myself, watch my hosts, watch my surroundings. The result had been that I had said almost nothing and had learned a lot. The elderly Japanese couple were wise people but I had never given them the chance to talk to me, I had always talked to them. It had been an amazing dinner.

And now, on this American road, I told myself to watch it. A car is a murderous instrument. I was, for the first time in my life, driving on an American highway. If I made a mistake I might cause a lot of trouble. I drove very carefully, minding the maximum speed of 60 miles an hour. The car ahead drove at exactly the same speed and for more than ten minutes I looked at the Afro haircut of the black woman driving it. I smiled at myself. It hadn't been so long ago, twelve or thirteen years maybe, that I had been proud of my wild driving. A man is nothing but an ever-changing combination of ever-changing habits. Wild driving is immoral. But what is "immoral"? I thought of the holy Buddhist priest, a master of Tantric Buddhism, who had smashed his fast Jaguar into a brick wall in a Scottish town, not so long ago. The holy priest had been very drunk at the time. An immoral man? Was Christ an immoral man when he cursed the fig tree?

Very deep questions. It might, meanwhile, be better to continue to drive carefully. Moral behavior is very convenient, it makes life easier, boring too perhaps, but easier. I shook my head. Perhaps I was, once again, on the wrong track. The old master had never preached morality to me. He had given me a *koan*. And Peter had never mentioned morality either. He had preached awareness. Although he hadn't used the word.

There had been the old clairvoyant American lady in Kyoto. Once I heard her talking to the old teacher. She had described a meeting of several disciples and the old man was listening to her. She started a new sentence. Peter was translating.

"And then I was aware. . . ."

The old man laughed. He got up and left the room. At the door he turned and looked at the old lady. "All these awarenesses!" he said, and disappeared into the corridor.

We laughed, but the old lady was tough. She bent her head and said, softly, to herself, but also to us, "I wasn't aware."

I watched it. I saw a man hitchhiking, standing next to a parked car. It took some trouble disengaging myself from the cluster of cars I was in, but finally I managed to get off the highway and I reversed towards the hitchhiker. He didn't see me and I pressed the horn. He came running towards me.

"Going to town?"

"Yes."

"My car is busted."

He got into the car and introduced himself. We shook hands and I mumbled my name. He was about thirty years old and his suit looked crumpled. A dirty shirt and no tie. He was carrying a small old suitcase tied with a piece of string. He smiled nervously.

"It's all right," he said.

He had a harelip which hadn't been operated upon properly; the cleft was still obvious.

"What do you mean?" I asked. "Why shouldn't it be all right?"

"I mean I am not going to hold you up."

He surprised me. The thought hadn't occurred to me.

"Why would you hold me up?"

"Well," he said, surprised as well, "for money of course."

"Do you need money?"

He shook his head and half closed his eyes. "Everybody needs money. But I've got enough on me. I only meant that I look a little like a bum and you might think that I am a robber who is using a broken-down car at the side of a road as an excuse to be picked up. It has happened before."

"Ah, America isn't a safe country. I had heard about it but I had forgotten. In Holland holdups aren't popular on the highway. Not yet anyway."

"Holland," the man said in a puzzled way. "A land of pastures and cows and water. My father was over there, during the war, he went there with the army. He said he had camped in a swamp and he always had diarrhoea, tigershit he called it. Ha ha."

"Ha ha," I said, "tigershit! That's good. I have associated Holland with a lot of things, but never with tigers. I'll remember it."

"Sorry," the man with the harelip said. "I didn't want to insult you, but I had to think of my father and he said that."

"Never mind," I said, "I think it's funny."

I had a tin of cigars in my sheepskin and offered him one. He took his time taking the paper ring off.

"And the people in Holland? Are they nice to each other?" my guest asked.

I thought about it. "Reasonably nice," I said in the end. "We all live on top of each other, eight hundred to the square mile I believe, and the roads are always full and the weather is like the bottom of an aquarium. You have to be nice to each other or you all go mad at the same time."

"A swampy heaven?" my friend asked.

"Well, heaven . . ." I said carefully.

"But you aren't frightened of each other?"

"No," I said.

"We are," the man with the harelip said. "We are frightened of each other. The whole lot of us. You see that bulge under my armpit?"

I saw the bulge. "A weapon?" I asked. He nodded. "Show me."

He gave me the weapon, an automatic pistol. The safety catch wasn't on and I slid it into place with my thumbnail.

"Never mind," the man said, "it isn't loaded. I did some target practice this morning and went through the lot. I knocked off a dozen bottles near my cabin. I live in the woods you know."

"Can you practice anywhere you like?" I asked.

"No," he said, "but everyone does. I don't think I know anyone who hasn't got a pistol, or a revolver, or something to kill with."

"So that's why you are frightened of each other?"

"There are other reasons as well," he said and choked on the smoke of his cigar.

It turned out that he knew the city well and he was very helpful. He showed me the supermarket where I could buy food and the store where Peter had ordered his circular saws and where I would have to take the axe without a handle. We had coffee in a restaurant where everything seemed to be made of paper. The cups and plates were of pressed paper, the hot dog tasted of paper, and the girl who banged our order on the table looked as if she had been cut out of a piece of soggy cardboard.

"The modern world," the man with the harelip said and pointed at a wall which had, once, been covered by plastic boards but most of them were torn and broken and we could see through it into the kitchen. We saw some longhaired young men with dirty, high white hats smashing lumps of minced meat on a large hot plate, and scraping them off again with pieces of tin attached to handles.

"I have worked in a place like this," my host said. "We have them all over the States. There were nine of us in the kitchen and seven were drug addicts. The heavy stuff. Their teeth were falling out and every now and then they would crack up and scratch the walls until the blood gushed out of their cuticles."

I studied his face. He looked scruffy but his eyes were clear and he had, in spite of the harelip, a strong mouth. He grinned.

"No. I smoked grass when I was young, but I have never been a junky. I used to drink a lot but that's over now, thanks to the AA. I'll always be an alcoholic, of course, but I have stopped drinking. If you would offer me a beer now I would say 'no thanks, I am an alcoholic.' That's the way I got off it, by admitting that I am an alcoholic."

"Would you like a beer?" I asked.

"No thanks," he said. "I am an alcoholic."

"Strange," I said. "Imagine that you wanted to introduce me to a nice young girl and I said, 'no thanks, I am a sexual maniac'." He laughed. "Funny," he said. "I'll remember it. But a girl isn't a glass of beer. A girl has a soul, and alcohol is a devil."

"You're a Christian?" I asked.

"No," he said, "but I believe in devils. Little ones. There are very few big devils around on Earth. Too easy for them. They send the little fellows here, to get some practice."

The idea was new to me and I prodded him on.

"Little devils. Their game is simple. You have to be very careful.

You give in a little and they get you a little. They are patient. They grab you slowly. First you can still make a few decisions, you can still say 'no' now and then, but gradually they take over. And when they have you they can do anything they like with you."

"And where do they take us?" I asked.

"To jail," the man with the harelip said, "or to a precipice. They don't have to shove you, you'll jump by yourself. You don't even know you are jumping."

"And where will you be then?" I asked. "In eternal hell?"

He gave me a very enquiring look. "I don't know. I don't think so. I believe there is a hell, but not forever. You'll probably be free again. Some day you'll find out where you are and you'll want to get out."

"And if you want to get out you can get out?" I asked.

He wobbled his head. "Something like that. I am not sure. I believe it. If you believe, you aren't sure. But perhaps you are right. You can leave when you really want to leave. Not before." He paid the bill and we said goodbye. A nice man, my friend with the harelip.

I did my shopping. The supermarket was just like the supermarket in Amsterdam. The cans and the packs and the jars were bigger, but that was the only difference I could see. The hardware store didn't look surprising either. The circular saws were ready for me and the man behind the counter fixed the axe in no time at all. I didn't have to pay; it was charged to Peter's account.

"You are part of *them*?" the man behind the counter asked.

"Who is *them*?" I asked.

"The commarde," the man said.

I had never heard of the word and asked him to explain.

"I don't know what it means," the man said. "That's what we call your place. A word somebody made up, I think. First we thought you people were communists but later we were told you were Buddhists. That's different. Anyway, I have been out there. Peter invited us all last summer, we had a nice day. He showed us around, we saw the farm, and that temple you have there with the seats.

He gave us a good meal too. I guess he had two hundred people out there, quite a crowd."

"Who did he ask? Anybody who wanted to come?"

"Yes. Anybody he deals with. The storekeepers and the postman and the banker. Anybody he knew here. Even the taxman went out there. And all the families too. The kids liked it. So did we."

I saw a knife I liked and bought it and he talked a little more.

"You share everything out there don't you?"

"I don't think so," I said, "everybody seems to make his own money. I am not sure though, I am only a visitor."

"It's a nice place," the man said, "but strange, nevertheless. I don't know how it works. Not that I mind really. That Peter is a good guy. He comes to visit sometimes. My son likes him."

He said "my son" in a peculiar way.

"Your son?"

He lowered his voice. "My son is retarded. And very close; he doesn't say much. But when Peter is here he will come into the store and they talk to each other. My son hasn't got too many words but Peter understands what he means."

"Ah," I said.

"Take your saws," the storekeeper said. He began to serve another customer and didn't say goodbye when I left.

I still had Peter's parcel to deliver and I stopped a man in the street to ask for directions. The man didn't answer, looked straight through me and kept on walking. Everybody is frightened of each other, the man with the harelip had said.

I looked around and noticed an old woman leaning on a stick. Old women don't scare so easily and I went up to her. She peered at the address on the parcel and showed me the way with her stick. She spoke with an accent.

"Aren't you American?" I asked.

Her eyes pierced through my skull. "You want to insult me young feller?"

"No madam," I said quickly. "I just thought you might come from another country."

"I am Russian," she said curtly.

"Have you been here long?"

"If you call sixty-six years long," she said and hobbled off.

"Thanks," I shouted but she didn't react.

America, the most powerful country in the world. An alcoholic with a harelip. A storekeeper with a retarded son. An old lady with a stick and a bad temper. And the world shakes with fear. Shadows in a play. I'll be damned if it isn't true, I thought. This can't be reality. This has to be a show of temporary forms, this isn't true, and if it isn't true there can never be any reason to be upset about anything. But do you have to sit under a tree for years on end to know that? Sure, sure, I thought. You have to sit for years under a tree to know that. To see that it isn't true is easy. But to see what *is* true will take some doing.

I found the address but not the man I wanted. His wife, or girl friend, a delicate girl in her early twenties, refused to take the parcel when I said it came from Peter.

"Robert will want to talk to you," she said, "you better give it to him yourself."

She told me where I could find him and, when she realized that I didn't know my way around the city, offered to give me a lift. I was surprised at the easy way in which she handled the large automobile and commented on it.

"You are in America," she said. "We learn to drive these wagons when we are still kids."

I thought of the war, the last days of the war. I was in Rotterdam, a fourteen-year-old boy watching a house in our street. There were SS officers in the house and they refused to surrender. The war was officially over and the German soldiery had obediently given in. Most of them had walked home, dressed in civilian clothes, or had been taken into custody by either the Allied army or the newly organized Dutch units. The SS were an exception, they knew they would be tried for war crimes.

Some twenty Dutch soldiers had made an attempt at taking the house. Two of them were dead, and a few wounded. The street was very quiet.

And then the Americans came. A tank rumbled past, followed

by another. Their guns blazed a few times. The house fell apart. When the smoke cleared an SS officer staggered out of the burning ruin. He collapsed in the street, close to the tanks. The boy who came out of the tank was the first American I ever saw. I jumped up and down and waved at him. He raised his tommy gun but lowered it again when he saw that I was a civilian. I was impressed. A boy, four or five years older than me but capable of driving a tank, of killing the all-powerful SS with a casual button touch.

"You are a very advanced people," I now said to the slight girl at the wheel of this large car.

She raised an eyebrow. "You're having me on," she said.

"No," I said. "I mean it."

She dropped me at the door of a workshop, waved and drove off. Robert was working on some intricate machinery inside and I introduced myself and gave him the parcel. He was tall, wide-shouldered with a crewcut which made him look like a film hero of the past.

"From Peter?" he asked.

"Yes," I said, "do you recognize the handwriting?"

"Not only the handwriting. I recognize you too. Peter has often told me about you, about the time you were together in Japan. You were very close to him once weren't you?"

"Yes," I said, "perhaps I was, but you never know with Peter. Were you close to him?"

Robert nodded. "Let's have lunch together," he said. "Are you free? We can talk while we eat."

I waited for him to wash his hands and followed him into the street.

I liked the restaurant he took me to, it was very different from the paper-place my harelipped friend had taken me to. This was an honest straightforward eating place with simple scrubbed tables and a fat lady with a jolly smile who took an interest in our choice.

"A drink?" Robert asked.

"If you have one."

He ordered two martinis and smiled at me.

"I don't normally drink during the day but this is a special occasion. You are a messenger from heaven, and should be well received."

"You think the commarde is a heaven?" I asked surprised.

He laughed. "No. I am not expressing myself well. It should lead to heaven. Purgatory I should have said."

"And what's this then? Your life here in this town?"

He laughed again. "Not hell, if that's what you mean. This is quite a pleasant place. An in-between place. I rest here."

We drank the martinis and he ordered another round.

"You had a difficult time over there?"

He told me about it while we ate. Gradually I gathered a picture of what his life in the commarde had been like. It was, in a way, an amusing story because he had got there by accident. He had been taken there, dragged even.

"I was a sick man. My mind, I mean. Really sick. I had lost all will to live. I was in bed, with a pain, a pain in my back somewhere, a very vague pain for I could never explain exactly where it was. The pain paralyzed me and I couldn't move. I lay in bed and looked at the ceiling. Going to the bathroom was a major effort."

"So?"

"So Peter got me out. He is a friend of a friend of mine and my friend met Peter in a New York street, by chance. Peter hardly ever leaves the commarde. They had lunch and my friend told Peter about me. He came to my room and pulled me out of bed. That same night he drove me out of New York. I never asked where he was taking me to. My back didn't hurt and I drove part of the way. We stopped for food a few times and we slept in the car. I never asked about our destination. I didn't care."

I could hardly believe it, they must have been driving together for days.

"You never asked?"

"No. I did as I was told. For months I moved like a machine. If he told me to work on the farm I worked on the farm. If he told me to meditate all night I meditated all night. If he didn't tell me anything I did nothing. I sat around and stared and smoked."

"You bought your own cigarettes?"

"No, Peter got them for me when he went shopping. I asked him to buy them."

"And?"

"Oh, I got out of my stupor. It took time but eventually I became reasonably normal again. I was in charge of the farm work for a while and I built my own cabin."

"So why did you leave?"

"Why did you leave the Japanese monastery?"

"I couldn't take it anymore. It seemed I was learning nothing and my *koan* died inside me."

Robert grinned. "The *koan*, eh?"

"You've got one?"

"Sure."

"Did you solve it?"

"We are not supposed to discuss *koans*," he said.

"Did you solve it?"

"No. I left. Peter put me in the limelight all the time. It seemed to me that he was spending as much time on me as he was spending on all the others together. He shouted ROBERT every time he opened his mouth. And he became bad-tempered as well. So one day I left."

"Have you been back at all?" I asked.

"Oh, several times. On visits. I took my girlfriend as well but she didn't like the place. She thinks I want to go back and leave her."

"But she could go as well?"

"She doesn't want to join them. I think she just wants to be with me."

"So are you sorry you left?"

He lent over and patted me on the head, a gesture he must have learned from Peter.

"Sure. But I learned a lot. I know how to look after myself. I might even start a family. I know how to work now, I am a mechanic, I've got my own workshop, I am even making some money. The world is very beautiful sometimes, the commarde taught me to see. I can see a plant, a tree, a bug."

We ate in silence for a while.

"Have a drink. Tomorrow Rohatsu starts, this is about your last chance to relax."

He surprised me. "You mean you remember the dates. You know when the important events are due?"

He smiled.

"I haven't left you see. I am still over there, every day. Those two years were the most important years of my life. Everything I do now is a direct consequence of what happened over there."

"So you will go back?"

He shook his head. "I don't know."

I drove back in a new cluster of cars, all keeping to the same speed. I talked to myself, aloud, to keep myself from falling asleep. My throat hurt; a touch of flu, brought with me from the Dutch swamps.

You are moving, between two points, and neither point can be defined.

From nowhere to nowhere?

Your view is spoiled by billboards, old, soggy, askew, advertising things you don't need.

The forest is bare and brittle.

You should feel sad but you feel warm inside.

You know it can happen any time now.

And if it never happens? Will that be bad?

You are surprised at your own conclusion. It won't be bad.

Eight

The blue jays

To meditate for ten hours a day, and to keep it up seven days. If you put it like that the exercise sounds terrible.

Perhaps it's all a matter of imagination. And with the right imagination almost anything can be managed. Just don't imagine too much, and don't imagine too far ahead. I got up at half past two that morning. The alarm was grinding away in its hoarse and irritable way.

We had put the alarm clock in a far corner of the cabin, well away from Rupert's sleeping bag and well away from my stack of horse blankets.

I didn't move and waited for Rupert. It's easy to think yourself into a position where you are always right. I told myself that I was a guest and Rupert a host. Hosts have duties. They have to get up first and make coffee. And when the coffee is ready the guest gets up. So I didn't move, but Rupert didn't move either.

The situation worried me and I began to shout. "Rupert, the alarm! The alarm!" Rupert groaned. I went on shouting.

"Yes," Rupert said, speaking slowly and very articulately, "I hear the alarm. But I am a little slow this morning." He was silent again and the alarm ground on.

"Rupert!"

"Yes."

He got up. At peace now I relaxed and rested my head against the wall. I watched Rupert liberating himself from his sleeping bag. Slowly he got to his feet, slowly he walked towards the alarm. I fell asleep again. The small metallic sound of the mug touching the floor next to my hip woke me up.

A few minutes later we were walking through the thick porridge of melting snow on the track. This sudden thaw didn't improve my discomfort. Snow and ice may be negative factors when you are living in a badly heated log cabin and have to spend a lot of time outdoors but they enhance the beauty of the landscape. Even snowstorms can be put up with. You think of the hermits in the Himalayas who meditate in the snow and of small groups of monks hiking through the passes, on their way to a holy and inaccessible place where, guided by a master, they will penetrate deeply into the mysteries of our existence. But what can you imagine when you tramp ankle deep, through a slow thick grey mass of matter? It even drizzled and my coat had become damp and heavy.

We arrived at the Zendo and I had difficulty in getting out of my boots. The disciples were crowding around me. I was hopping about on one foot when a fat girl bumped into me and I fell over an elderly looking man who was trying to untangle his shoelaces. Nobody said anything. The silence had started. For one week we would only use our voices when something of importance had to be expressed.

On the way to the Zendo Rupert had left me behind. He was the jikki jitsu, the meditation leader, and had to get to the Zendo well before the others. I saw him now at the end of the hall, perched high on his cushions, motionless, the wooden clappers ready to give the signal for the first period.

I had promised myself not to think ahead. This was the first period of a bunch of seven. Seven times twenty-five minutes, six short rests of five minutes each. Three and a half hours in all. Three and a half hours can be managed, especially if you can chop them up. And two periods would be very easy as they would be spent, partly, in walking to and from Peter's house. And there would be the excitement of the new *koan*.

The Zen sect I had blundered into in Japan belonged to the Rinzai school. Rinzai is known for its extensive use of *koans* but there are also other Zen methods. Soto-Zen for instance hardly uses the *koan*. And, as Soto priests will point out, *koans* aren't really necessary. The Buddha didn't use one when he sat down under his tree. The only reason (the Soto priests say) that the Rinzai training uses *koans* almost continuously is because Rinzai attracts intellectual, or merely restless, minds. To force a restless mind to sit still and concentrate on the great "Nothing" which causes and explains all phenomena is impossible. So the Rinzai disciple has to be tricked, and he is tricked by giving him *koans* to solve. With a *koan* he is under the impression that he has "something to do."

Whether there is any truth in this criticism I wouldn't know. It may be that the rebuff, like many rebuffs, is born from jealousy. It might be possible that the Soto priests felt inferior. Many Rinzai people became famous in China and Japan. They had brilliant minds. And the Soto people, who risked falling into apathy by their very stillness, may have been tempted to sneer at them.

Each path, each method, attracts its own type. I had, without knowing it, knocked on a Rinzai gate when I made my first contact with Buddhism in Kyoto. And now, thinking back, I wasn't sorry. The new *koan* excited me. Excitement, of course, is a surface sensation, and has neither depth nor value, but it would help me through this week.

So, using my imagination, I assured myself that this week would be very easy as I climbed onto my cushions and settled down. The signal hadn't sounded yet and I had a chance to look around. I had to do it quickly for nobody likes to be stared at, especially in meditation hall. My fat friend with the walrus moustache sat next to me, the slight girl was on the other side. Three girls faced me, two of them looked almost happy; they sat well in the double lotus. One of them impressed me, she had a round placid face and reminded me of a primitive Buddha statue on my bookshelf in Amsterdam, a simple figure expressing no more than quietness. The third girl sat badly. She was very tall and she had twisted her legs with difficulty. Her face was set in a grim expression of dogged courage. She would get through the week if it killed her. I had met her on the highway, a few days before and we had talked a little. She was new to this and was dreading Rohatsu. I had tried to cheer her up and she had smiled at me.

"I know what you are going through," I thought now but wondered at the same time. Perhaps we never know what the other goes through. The company of the four females close to me made me feel warm. The American school allows women to join in the training. In principle the Japanese school does too but females are never allowed in the Zendos. They have to sit in a room by themselves, somewhere in the main temple of the monastery, and the monks will run up to them sometimes and whack them with their sticks. There are other discriminating rules but the core of the training, *sanzen*, the meeting with the master, is the same for everybody and women can, and do, albeit rarely, become masters.

Peter, fortunately, had done away with all discrimination, and I was sure that the old teacher approved. So here we were, twenty-four men, twelve women, happily mingled in the same ordeal.

Rupert hit his clappers and a small nervous shock ran down my spine. I bundled all the energy I could muster and dived, as far as I could.

Ten minutes passed and I heard the rustling of a silk kimono. The master was with us. Peter walked slowly, making his round. At the second round he corrected our attitudes. I hadn't bent my head and he gently pushed it so that my nose pointed down a little. With a straight neck sleep attacks easily and concentration dwindles giving way to circling dreams. With the chin down there seems to be a surge of power.

My fat friend attracted all Peter's attention. He shoved and pushed, stepping back even like a sculptor studying his creation. My neighbor even had to undo his hands and clasp them again. No detail was overlooked.

The slight girl was next. She had already had a turn but she had slumped forward again and Peter came back to her, shaking her by the shoulders and pushing her back until her spine assumed the right position.

When he had finished with us he walked up to the altar and spoke.

"This is the beginning of a long week. Do your best and keep at it. Rohatsu is a rare gift, as life itself is a rare gift. Don't dream. Forget whatever you think you have understood, forget your attainments. Work on your *koan*, and on nothing else. Find your real self."

He spoke slowly without raising his voice. He had been, earlier

78

in his life, a teacher of singing, and he knew how to make his voice reach into the furthest corner of the Zendo.

I heard the kimono rustle past me again and the Zendo's door closed with the dry sound of wood touching wood. The man in charge of the tea came past, carrying his heavy kettle. We raised our cups, taking them from their fixed positions behind our cushions. We drank when Rupert's bell told us to drink. When the bell rang again we replaced the cups. We didn't have to think, everything was regulated, right down to the minute. All we had to do was concentrate on the *koan*. Very simple.

And difficult, impossible. While I tried to avoid my thoughts and return to my *koan* the minutes ebbed away and the bell sounded. My leg cramped and I climbed down, glad to be able to stand for a while. In the Zendo no unnecessary movement is allowed. During meditation you sit, and when there is a break you sit. But during the breaks you may, if you absolutely have to, stand. Or you may leave the hall and move about a little outside. But, whatever you do, you do it quietly. You don't look at each other. You don't clear your throat or blow your nose. You may sneeze or cough because even Zen discipline accepts that sneezing and coughing cannot always be stopped at will.

The morning passed quickly. Twice I went into the master's room and heard the little bell ring and found myself outside again. I would pass the *koan* that week, and others as well, but there was no merit to be gained. These were the "little" *koans*, satellites of the "big" one which had opened me up somewhat. The little *koans* might widen the crack, or not. I seemed to understand the direction I was following. Seemed, no more. A master is a master and I couldn't really know what he was guiding me into. I fully expected him to suddenly turn round and snap at me, pushing me back into my original bewilderment. I trod very wearily, with pricked ears. I wasn't going to be caught if I could help it. Meanwhile I knew that my effort was useless, if he wanted to push me back he would push me back. He was thoroughly at home on my level, for he had been there himself, for years and years. And I couldn't even visualize *his* level.

The blue jays

The *koans* he gave me weren't new to me. I had heard them in Japan. The monks had mentioned them and I had run across them in Zen literature. Some of them Peter himself had given me, ten years before in Kyoto, casually, while we were working in the garden together, or washing up, or shopping.

I had thought about these *koans* before, perhaps even worked on them without knowing that I was working on them. But now I was pushed right in, rubbed through them with my nose. The extraordinary questions, phrases, statements, caught me and I gave faltering answers which were refused, again and again, until suddenly, usually while I was walking about outside, on the highway or the tracks, the answer appeared and would be accepted at the next *Sanzen*, to be followed immediately by a new, idiotic or impossible, exercise.

In one way these *koans* were all alike. "Solving" them really didn't mean all that much. The insight they touched was far too deep. I knew that if I could break through even part of one of them, I would be safely on "the other shore," the state of transcendence which the Buddha claimed to have reached. But I wasn't transcending anything, I was merely sniffing at these bits of supreme wisdom, sniffing carefully, and nervously.

Sanzen is an extraordinary method. There is no conversation, no discussion at all. Nothing is reasoned out. The question is strange and the answer is just as strange. Question and answer are of the same kind. No point of view can be defended. There is only *one* answer and the disciple knows when he gives the wrong one. There is never any surprise when the teacher rings his bell and the interview is over. And when the disciple has the right answer he knows that it will be acknowledged. The teacher can't refuse, and the disciple doesn't even worry about a possible refusal. There is no examination, perhaps the interview is a direct meeting of minds. And there is no hurry, no way of forcing the answer. The only way to find it is through concentration, if it doesn't pop up by itself the concentration must be renewed. There is no other way.

The *koans* I was given originate in China, the China of a thousand years ago, from the time that masters lived casually with their dis-

ciples in an out-of-the-way place in the mountains. The questions
occurred freely, at odd moments. The disciples meditated in caves,
cabins, or in the forest. The *koans* began to live by themselves and
were passed on, from master to master, and when the disciple became a master he used the *koans* he had worked on himself. And
when the monasteries began the *koans* moved into their discipline,
they were bundled up and became a method with different stages.

And I, man of today, had to use these antiquities and found that
they worked, and that my mind wasn't all that different from the
mind of an ancient Chinese. And like the ancient Chinese I had to
learn to express my answers in core-language. If I added anything,
a gesture, a word, an explanation, the answer was refused. Only if
I gave the bare bone the master would smile. The marrow of the
bare bone. Nothing more. No conjugation of the verb. No subject.
No object. No projection of the self. Why project a shadow which
only lasts a moment?

No self. I began to get used to the idea. The shape walking about
in the melting snow of a faraway country was nothing but a temporary transparent changing figure. An apparent identity, nothing
more. A vehicle. A cloudy spook on his way from a non-real beginning to a just as non-real end. Or rather, I thought I could accept
it. But I knew that this apparent identity would, at the drop of a
soft hat, speak up for itself, lose its temper, be jealous or greedy,
or filled with fear. It would probably quake if it cut its finger; a
free spirit can be made into mincemeat and it will smile right
through the treatment. I meant to get that far.

But meanwhile I kept on rejoicing about the event of a mug of
coffee during the longer intervals when we could return to our
cabins, or the cigarette I would smoke on my way back to Rupert's
camp, or dinner. The breaks became very important. We had an
hour and a half at midday and another similar period later in the
day. And at nine o'clock it was all over. And although I did my
feeble best not to look forward to these islands of liberty, I did.

By 9:15 p.m. I would be dug in, separated from the harsh world
by my stack of blankets, and would tumble into a dreamless sleep,
the most happy situation, according to Socrates, a man can reach.

The blue jays

It might be, I thought every time I slid into sleep, that Socrates was right.

An extra affliction interfered with my well-being. Like most of the disciples I had caught a cold. My chest felt as if it was filled with ground glass. When I meditated the snot ran into my moustache and across my lips. There was nothing I could do to stop it. Waving a handkerchief was, of course, right out of the question but even the merest sniffing would raise a shout from the jikki's seat. "Let it run," Rupert would shout and the only comfort the disciples could feel was that Rupert's cold seemed as bad as theirs.

Dreamless sleep is the end of it all. There is nobody left and "nobody" is incapable of anything. If "I" am not there "I" cannot suffer, feel, worry, complain or even feel uncomfortable.

But it wasn't the final goal. I refused to believe that Buddhism aims at total extermination. "The other shore" would have to be very different from the state of dreamless sleep, and if after all, it should turn out to be identical I would refuse to accept it and get off it, cursing the Buddha and the Zen masters. Meanwhile I sat and shivered inside my jersey and sheepskin. I was running a temperature and the pain in my legs crept up, gradually, until it reached my shoulders. My skull pricked. The very tall girl opposite had her troubles as well. She sneezed every few minutes and her legs got so stiff that she could hardly get off her seat during the intervals. The thought that her long legs were filled with pain made me feel close to her and when I saw her on the highway I walked next to her dangling shape, without words but with an occasional sneeze of my own to keep her company.

The Buddha refused to answer questions dealing with the end of human or general existence. And if he did answer he would say that there would be no end, but that there would be no no-end either. I believed, for the sake of convenience, that it would turn out to be an existence in other dimensions, of an order beyond my brain. This belief seemed more pleasant than the idea of complete destruction.

This pleasing thought was confirmed, eight times a day, during my walks, by a pair of birds. Rupert told me they were "blue jays," a larger variety of the Dutch jay, and colored a bright blue. Jays aren't nice birds; they feed, in spring, on the eggs and young of other birds but they live an honest life in winter, feeding on scraps of food provided by the forest. But even then they are not very pleasant. I would scatter crumbs and other leftovers near Rupert's cabin but I meant to feed the other smaller birds as well. They never had a chance, the jays took charge of the feeding ground.

Every time I watched the jays I became convinced that life is an unbelievable miracle and that its ultimate end will be just as miraculous. The jays were a manifestation of the miracle to come. And not only the jays but also the bare trees all around me with their lovely combinations of thin twigs, and also the brook which wound its way through the forest and which was led past the highway through thick rusty pipes. At the end of one of these pipes the clear water streamed quickly and formed eddies and the frost, which had started again, made icicles in the mouth of the pipe. As a child I had never been impressed by fairy tales believing them to be silly inventions to amuse or frighten kiddies but now I began to believe in them and I could easily imagine a fairy queen living in the pipe, directing a gorgeous court and listening to jazz played by gnomes. Every time I stopped at the pipe I fell in love with the fairy queen, a small sexy Bodhisattva, an intelligent and enticing entity.

Somebody touched my shoulder. I turned round and saw my fat neighbor with the walrus moustache. He had pulled the hood of his duffelcoat over his head and a pair of lively eyes looked at me from under the rim.

"My name is Edgar," my fellow-disciple said.

I said my name and we shook hands. The silence still ruled and we shouldn't really have spoken to each other but rules are no fun unless they are broken occasionally.

"You smoke nice cigarettes," Edgar said. "I smell them every time I pass you on the road, they drive me crazy. Give me one."

I had a spare pack in my pocket and put it in his hand. He thanked me elaborately.

"You shouldn't thank me," I said. "Smoking is a bad habit. It will narrow your veins and clog your blood and if you go on you may lose a limb."

Edgar lit a cigarette and looked at me through the smoke. The silence had returned.

I put up a hand and returned to the cabin. On the way I thought about Edgar. We had spent some eighty hours sitting next to each other. I had heard him groan and curse under his breath. At the end of each period he would say, "Ah, *good*," very softly. Only I could hear him. He had no other neighbor, his seat was right at the end.

You are not alone.

There are others, on their way on the same track.

Travellers from nowhere to nowhere, on their way from nothing to nothing.

The track may be narrow and steep and boring and frightening but everybody walks on it.

You are not alone but linked to everything around you.

Nine

The white mouse

The eighth of December is the birthday of the Buddha's insight, the insight which he claimed under the famous Bodhi-Tree of India. Someone must have made a note of the day. I would have liked to meet him. A thin dried-out monk perhaps, with a pencil behind his ear and a block of lined notepaper under his arm.

All Zen monks celebrate the insight's birthday and all Zen monasteries know the week of Rohatsu, the seven days preceding festivity. And now it was the last day, the seventh. I felt somewhat more comfortable on my seat. My troubles were nearly over. Twice I had been sent out of the hall for half an hour, because I had moved. Once I had been severely spoken to, for lagging behind.

At mealtimes we ate in Peter's house, ruled by the jikki's bell. We marched out in a goose file, marched into the house, sat down at the bell's command, ate at the bell's command, washed our bowls at the bell's command. And then we walked back to the Zendo, the jikki leading the file. I had maneuvered myself into the tail of the line. I didn't like this regimental behavior and as the last of the line I could regulate my own speed of walking. But my behavior had been noticed. I was accused of reluctance, and rightly so. And I had mended my ways. From that moment on I walked with the others and ran with the others. We were in it together and I had accepted the rules.

Still, at the back of my mind, I feebly protested. I had joined the training, once in Japan, and now again in America, to meet a mystery, face to face. The people of Zen had seemed free to me, like the characters of Cold Mountain,* two grotesque little men

---

* *Cold Mountain: A Hundred Poems by the T'ang Poet Han-Shan*, translated by Burton Watson (London: Cape; New York: Columbia University Press, 1970).

guffawing in the wilderness inscribing poems on trees and rocks."
I wondered what men like Han-Shan and his friend Shih-te would
think of having their meals at the command of a bell, rung by a
disciplinarian.

Both the Japanese and the Americans have a military reputation,
they wave flags and wear uniforms. The Dutch may be different;
our heroes, if we have any, are bearded pirates with a single earring
who will take their time before obeying an order. They will discuss
it with a bottle of jenever on the table and then, maybe, they will
do something altogether different. When the German army overran
our country the Dutch responded with refusal and, eventually, with
aggression. Even our Nazis who joined the SS had to be treated
differently and would only fight if they were allowed some individual freedom.

But my surrender paid off. Nobody worried me during the last
few days. The quick run to the house relaxed the muscles of my
legs and I was sitting without pain. Pain was replaced by my old
enemy: sleep. I fell asleep constantly and had to rush out during
the breaks to rub my face with snow.

I had asked myself how it would be if this exercise were pro-
longed for life. Everything has been done before on Earth, and
even today there must be monasteries where monks sit for ten
hours a day, every day. The Catholic Church has nuns and monks
who spend their lives in meditation, locked away in their cells, and
Tibetan Buddhism and the Yoga religion have hermits who, vol-
untarily, retire behind brick walls with only a small hole through
which a meal is passed, once every other day.

In the Zendo, just within my field of vision, an elderly man with
a bald head had attracted my attention. All movements in the Zendo
were limited by protocol but it seemed as if this man's movements
were even more restricted than those of the others. Whenever it
was time to leave the hall he climbed off his seat with the rhythm
of a puppet, even his breathing seemed mechanical. Then he would
open the sliding door of the cabinet underneath his seat and take
out his windbreaker. He would put it on but there was something
wrong with the left sleeve and he would give it an irritable look,
shake the sleeve, and finally manage to get his arm into it. The

repetition became monotonous and I knew exactly what to expect but even so I would find myself asking nervously *what* he was trying to do this time. And, day after day, I would think, "Ah, of course, he is going to get his windbreaker from the cabinet."

If the exercise, instead of seven days, had lasted seven weeks this endless repetition might have made me scream. As it was I was becoming subject to tensions.

Tensions in the Zendo are normal. In Japan I had witnessed how some of the monks, especially the young ones, could not bear the stress. Egged on by the master and the senior monks, driven relentlessly to break their *koans*, they rebelled, without probably wanting to rebel. I had seen how a monk, on his way to *sanzen*, had grabbed one of the altar's supporting poles and refused to go on.

The head monk had come into action immediately. He jumped down from his seat, lithe as a panther, and rushed at the monk. On the way he grabbed a *kesaku*, the stick the monks hit each other with during meditation periods, and using it as a lever, forced the arms of the monk free from the pole. Helped by another senior monk he simply picked the little fellow up and carried him to the *sanzen*-room. There, as I was told later, they dumped him on the mat in front of the master's seat, and waited in the corridor for the interview to come to an end.

I began to think that I would be capable of similar behavior. What particularly bothered me was that I was working on two *koans* at the same time. I had my own, given to me by the master, but I had run into another.

According to tradition Zen masters will deliver "*teishos*," short lectures, on every day of Rohatsu. Peter had selected a special *koan* for these *teishos* and confronted us with it seven times. *Teishos* were given in his house, in the large sitting-room, which could just about hold us all. He would wait for us on his knees, dressed in his formal robe, behind a low table on which we saw a thin book, a book I remembered from his temple in Japan. The book contained a collection of famous *koans*, dating back to the Middle Ages. We would come in quietly, kneel down and face him. He would sweep the room with his eyes, take a deep breath and recite his choice.

The white mouse

The *koan* was long:

A Zen master is old and ill. He has been in bed for a few days and a monk comes to visit him. The monk enquires after the master's health. The master answers that it will be strange if his body is not carried to the graveyard within three days.

The monk is silent but the master sits up and says:

"Buddhas with moon-faces. Buddhas with sunfaces." The story is noted down and a later Zen master comments as follows:

"Very fresh, very fresh. But too kind. That old teacher wants to make things too easy for his disciples. He reminds me of a nursery-maid."

This *koan* hit us collectively, huddled close together in the stuffy room. We looked at the master who had closed his eyes. The lines in his face were deep, not a muscle in his body moved.

"Buddhas with moon-faces. Buddhas with sunfaces." What was I to make of a sentence like that?

But the *koan* began to fascinate me. The girl opposite me in the Zendo had a moon-face. The little Buddha statue on my bookshelf at home had a moon-face. I began to think that moon-faces were of the utmost importance, I had to find out what they meant.

The moon itself helped to push me to the edge of my sanity. Every night it sat in the sky, round and full, suspended in its great emptiness. I imagined that I could hear the sound of the moon, a shrill ghostly note piercing the silent landscape. It touched my bones while I walked through my white world.

Peter commented on the *koan*. He mentioned the fact that Buddhas with moon-faces live for a day and a night. Buddhas with sunfaces live for eighteen hundred years. Perhaps the point of the *koan* had to do with Time. But I didn't want to work on it, I had my own *koan*, which I carried into *sanzen* five times a day.

One evening I stopped on the path to Rupert's cabin and leaned against a tree. I had the moon full in my face. I had found the answer to my *koan* and I didn't want to accept it. It would take me further than I was prepared to go. I was shaking my head and laughing at myself. I would have to go further. The old teacher had been right when he spoke to me in my dream. "Your personality will crumble away, until there is nothing left." Whatever had I let myself in for?

I seriously thought of running away. I could have walked to the nearest store and telephoned for a taxi. I could probably have caught a plane that very night. But I shook the thought off and walked back to the cabin.

I think the Buddha's smile saved me. The Buddha, at the end of his long effort, smiled.

My father had taken me once to a museum in Rotterdam. I must have been six or seven years old. It was the first time I had seen a Buddha statue. It smiled.

"Why does he smile, father?"

My father had ruffled my hair.

"Why, father?"

"Perhaps you'll find out one day."

I still wanted to find out.

The seventh, last day. Tradition has it that Rohatsu ends in a party. Rupert had made no preparations for the party so I assumed we would be invited out. I was looking forward to the last sound of the bell. It would die away slowly, we would remain in our seats for another minute and wait for the jikki to leave the hall and then, for the last time, we would form up and leave in an orderly manner. But outside we would be free, free to laugh and to joke and slap each other on the shoulders. And then we would be off somewhere, to eat and drink.

The last period came and I did my best not to waste it. The sudden voice of the jikki disturbed me.

"Tonight there will be no party," Rupert said. "Peter wants us to continue the silence until tomorrow morning. We are all expected at the old teacher's grave at 9: a.m. After that there will be a communal breakfast."

He coughed. I waited for the rest of the message but the silence had been dropped back into the Zendo. Edgar, my neighbor, blew through his moustache.

"Good day," I thought. "No party. Terrible."

89

But when the wave of disappointment had passed I grinned. No party. So what? I didn't really care about the party. There were other pleasant events to think of. Rohatsu was over and I would be able to sip coffee at my ease, nice strong coffee with condensed milk from a tin. And dive underneath my blankets afterwards. And sleep late the next morning. I wouldn't have to get up until eight. And after breakfast I would go out for a walk through the forest or to the beach. I would be able to look at the horseshoe crabs and feed the blue jays. And I had a good conscience. I had done my best, it could have been better, of course, but even so, I had really tried this time.

I estimated that we had another five minutes to go, and went back into my concentration.

The familiar rustling of Peter's silk kimono brought me back into the hall. He had opened Rohatsu, now he would close it. I was listening, no doubt he would choose the right words. He had reached the altar and turned round to face us. "I want to tell you the story of the little white mouse." A tremendous happiness surged through me. *The White Mouse*. Could he have picked a better title? The minute animal with its long tail who lives in a glass box and digs tunnels through sawdust and who, at the summit of his activity, will run in a wheel made out of cigarbox-wood. When Peter said "the white mouse" I knew that my doubts about the discipline and the general training I had been subjected to were without substance. I was, after all, in the world of Han-Shan and his friend Shih-te, the crazy little fellows who ran about on their Cold Mountain, a thousand years ago. I had, when I went to Japan, done what I should have done.

With the speed of lightning a number of scenes were reenacted in my mind, the first signs of the liberation which this adventure would eventually bring about. I remembered how, as a child, I had known that the excitement, fears and worries the grownups of my immediate environment went in for, had no real foundation. I knew it in flashes but the others would always manage to convince me that I was wrong and once again I would feel guilty or fearful or both.

Human nature has no real connection with guilt and fear but is free. I also knew that this discovery had nothing to do with any specific religion, not even with the smile of the Buddha statue. The Buddha discovered what had been known long before him. The religion founded on his experience had nothing to do with the sudden flash of liberation which I felt that evening in the Zendo. I understood now why the master in the Kyoto temple had refused to accept my application to become a Buddhist. To limit oneself to a fanatic acceptance of any creed blocks the way out.

I remembered how the old teacher, during the more than twenty years of his mastership, had refused to use the words Buddhism or Zen and he had always smiled, surprised, when a disciple would quote the Buddha to prove a point.

"A little white mouse," Peter repeated.

"In Japan a white mouse is a good omen. When you see a white mouse you are in for a bit of luck. It is a sign of health, much money, success.

"One day a father and his son were having their evening rice in their small house.

" 'Father,' the son said, 'don't suddenly look round now but behind you we have a little guest, somebody who will bring us luck.'

"The father, carefully, looked over his shoulder. He saw a little white mouse.

"Father and son smiled. Quietly they observed the mouse, running to and fro on the rice straw-mats.

"But then the mouse shook itself and, in one movement, became an ordinary grey mouse. A grey mouse who, accidentally, had fallen into the flour tin."

Peter looked at us, one by one.

"Don't be like the little white mouse. It has been a hard week. A difficult exercise. If you shake yourself now you will be as grey as you were when you started Rohatsu. Watch it, and stay white. One day you may really be white."

He bowed and left the Zendo. Rupert rang his bell for the last time.

Perhaps you have had *satori* now. The great experience the Zen books talk about.

Does it matter what exactly you have experienced?

Of course it doesn't.

Nothing matters.

Satori doesn't matter either.

Forget the word.

Live as if you have never heard it.

Ten

Moon-faced Buddha

The large rock shading the old teacher's grave looked stark against its background of fir trees. The day was clear, there was almost no wind. I stood alone, gazing at the rock, thinking of the old master as I had last seen him, very neat in his freshly laundered grey kimono, quiet and very strong.

Peter had picked the right place. The rock expressed austerity and solitude and the firs were perfect, reminding me of the colors of the Zen gardens, greys and many greens.

I had come on my own, ten minutes early. I had wanted to be alone with the old Japanese priest who had once accepted me into his sect and teaching. But I wasn't the only one standing near the rock. Some twenty feet away stood Rupert, with his hands behind his back and behind me I felt the presence of Edgar, the fat enigmatic disciple who blew through his walrus moustache and said "Ah, *good*" at the end of each period. Neither of them had known the old teacher but they were as close to him as I, or, perhaps, as far away.

Another disciple arrived, a tall man, some thirty years old, who looked as if he had been put together in a hurry. He must have bought his clothes in a store dealing in discarded army clothes and he wore a Castro cap with earflaps. I had seen him and his thin long goatlike beard before but I had never talked to him. He stopped at some distance, faced the grave, and froze. The four of us spent at least five minutes together, then the others arrived and gradually filled the open space in the forest.

I felt attracted to the tall man in the army clothes, he seemed very familiar as if we had been to school together, and I meant to make contact with him later. I felt that a meeting might be very fruitful, might clarify some of the many riddles. Riddles, I thought despondently, too many riddles. He is plunging his way through them, and so am I. He looks as bewildered as I must look to others. And yet we share the same arrogance, for he must be as determined as I am to reach "the other shore." I stopped my thoughts at the word "arrogance." Perhaps I had found a clue. To strive for something, no matter what it is, is egocentric behavior. To strive means to grab. Perhaps I shouldn't grab.

The old teacher had told me about the man under the apple tree. First he grabbed at the apples and every now and then he would get one, but they were small and they were crushed in his hand. Then he changed his attitude. He just stood under the tree and stopped jumping. He merely held up his hands and when the apples were ripe they fell into his hands, and there were so many apples that he didn't know what to do with them and gave them away.

"So I must wait," I thought, "like I am waiting here in the snow. And while I am waiting I can do the best I can."

Buddhism indicates the possibility of many lives, a sea of illusionary time. Whatever it is I want will come, when it wants to come. All I have to do is be there when it comes. And then I can give it away.

Sure, I thought. Very nice. But meanwhile there is the urgency of the *koans*. Whenever I pass one there is another. An endless supply of riddles, all to be solved on the spot. Peter doesn't approve of his disciples hanging about patiently waiting.

I saw the old master again. I faced him, kneeling on the mat in front of his seat. Being a small man his eyes were at the level of mine. We were no more than three feet apart. Once again I hadn't known the answer to the *koan* and he was going to ring his little bell to indicate that the interview was over. Desperately I stopped his hand.

"How is it possible," I said in my broken slow Japanese, "that we are so far apart. Here I am, three feet away from you. But you are out of reach. I haven't the slightest idea how I can get to you."

He watched me quietly. His eyes, looking like almost black beads, twinkled under the heavy tufted eyebrows.

"You are where I am," the master said, "and that's where you have always been. You know already what you want to know and you are where you want to be. There is no difference between us. You are a Buddha, I am a Buddha."

He shook his bell and I made my bows. I knew, when I walked back to the meditation hall, that he was right but also that the distance was still there. Undoubtedly I was possessed of the Buddha nature, and not just me but everybody and everything. The blades of grass at the side of the path, the animals, the bugs, and all beings, dead or alive, in the entire universe. The evil spirits, the sadists of the concentration camps, the exploiters, the corrupt judges, the generals setting fire to villages, all have the Buddha nature. A beautiful truth which I could, intuitively, comprehend. But to comprehend is not enough. I would have to bridge the gap between the master and myself. I would have to make it in one desperate leap. And the only way I would be able to do that would be by giving up.

I was cold. We were all there now. The elderly man with the bald head arrived on a stretcher, he had twisted his foot on the last morning of Rohatsu and Edgar had driven him to the hospital. He wasn't too badly hurt but he wouldn't be able to walk for a few weeks. Two of the stronger boys were carrying the stretcher and they put it down gently, close to the rock. We were still waiting for Peter. There was nothing to do and I began to concentrate on my *koan*. In this type of training there is never any boredom, there is always something to do.

A Tibetan monk in Holland whose papers weren't in order and who was facing arrest and a period in jail laughed at me once when I worried about him. "No need to worry," he said, "in jail I can meditate." Fortunately he didn't go to jail, the border-police gave him a visa.

I remembered Peter in Kyoto. He had invited me to go to the cinema with him, the film was supposed to be a nature film but he had made a mistake and we were watching gangsters kidnapping a beautiful virgin. He wanted to leave but stayed when he saw that I was enjoying the movie. I looked at him after a while and saw that he was meditating, he had managed to get into full lotus on the uncomfortable narrow seat. He would do the same if he had to wait his turn at the barbershop.

It was very quiet near the grave. Occasionally somebody coughed. A woman I had seen in the Zendo had brought her two children, a boy of five and a girl of three years old. They stood next to me and fidgeted.

A rhythmical crackling announced Peter's arrival. He was wearing a silk kimono and the cords, attached to the large white ring of the Zen school. Three of the younger disciples followed him. The first carried a bundle of incense sticks, the second a teapot, the third a teacup on an ornamental tray.

I grimaced. This formal religious approach was well outside my scope. I had always believed the ceremonies to be useless. The ancient masters in China, the originals living in their mountain camps with a few disciples would have done without them. I shrugged. Who cares? If Peter wanted a ceremony I would be part of it.

And perhaps I was enjoying it. Psychoanalysis might tell me why I didn't like ceremonies. Perhaps some traumatic association with Christmas parties and the Dutch Santa Claus celebration. This ceremony might very well have a purpose. It was a symbol of respect and I certainly respected the old master. Thanks to him this commarde had been born. The old master has passed on his insight. He could have taken his insight into the mountains and lived there by himself, blissfully, as other holy men have done and the flame would have died with his body. But the old master had chosen the tiresome discipline of a monastic life where he had to see his disciples, one by one, very early in the morning. He had helped them on their various ways, had guided them, and cheered them up when they thought they were stuck and had snapped at them and hit them when they took the wrong turning. He had kept it up till he died. And one of the men he had taught was Peter, the man now kneeling at the rock and lighting the first incense stick and planting it in the snow.

Peter invited us to follow his example. My turn came and I lit the stick with my lighter. I bowed, prostrated myself in the snow, got back onto my knees and planted it. The ceremony didn't take much time, everybody except the two children had taken part in it.

Peter called the children. The girl hid herself under her mother's coat, but the boy, after some hesitation, came forward. Peter lit the incense for him.

The boy wanted to, and didn't want to. There isn't much difference between children and grown-ups. The same feelings live in both. A child knows, often very consciously, that he walks about on a very strange planet, that he is, temporarily, dealing with certain types of miracles and that these miracles hide a purpose and that he has to discover the purpose. An adult is easily stopped in his quest, a child is not. But a child is held back by the adults around him who rule his life and frustrate him as a matter of habit.

I was glad Peter hadn't forced the girl to take part in the ceremony.

The boy wanted to join in, he had accepted the incense stick and was turning it about, not sure what he was going to do with it. Peter was of no help at all. Suddenly the boy made up his mind, he shrugged his right shoulder, waving the arm attached to it, walked to the rock, bowed and prostrated his small body. I saw that the incense had touched his hand and burned it. The boy pulled a face but didn't cry out.

When he walked back to his mother he passed Peter. Peter patted him on the head and the boy lost his tenseness and smiled. The party started with the smile of the little boy.

I had some trouble holding on to myself. I wanted to get off the holy ground, cross the bridge and dance about. Enough is enough. I had been quiet for an entire week and lived with shadows instead of human beings. The man with the goat beard was the first I met on the other side of the bridge. We embraced.

"Yes, yes," he said. My attention was caught by Edgar who was thumping me on the shoulder.

"Have a cigarette," he said.

—

Later, when the plane had begun its final descent towards Amsterdam airport, I remembered the man with the goat beard. I hadn't seen him again and had forgotten him. Perhaps he had only joined the commarde for Rohatsu, he may have been one of Peter's "outside" disciples, people living in other parts of the States who could only manage to visit the settlement for a few weeks at the time. Perhaps he had caught a plane home immediately after the ceremony. And perhaps the man with the goat beard didn't exist at all. But I knew him well.

When I entered Peter's sitting-room I felt shy. Five times a day, seven days long, I had knelt in that room preparing myself for *sanzen*. From that room I had taken my jump at the master. The room had seemed ghostlike to me, the green color of the carpet was a hellish green, the jute-material which covered the walls had been the boundary of my little "I" and even the dusty grand piano appeared as a monster of which the keys would have been the teeth.

But now the room had changed. The always empty grate now contained a crackling merry fire and every corner had its fat burning candles, stuck in huge green bottles. Peter, the guide to the big secrets, the grim master, the manifestation from the beyond and the Absolute had become a pleasant man, sitting somewhere on the floor behind a plate of thick pancakes and with a glass in his hand. I was given a glass as well and Edgar filled it for me from a gigantic jar. I tasted orange juice, glowing with vodka. I took a huge sip. Behind the bottle I saw Edgar's grinning face.

"That's it?" he asked.

"That's it," I said.

I looked about me. The girl with the round face sat next to me, the moon-faced Buddha from my bookshelf, I told her that I had her in my apartment, on the bookshelf, but she didn't know what I was talking about. I had to explain it, which was a pity. I didn't want to explain anything. I tried to explain that as well, which was another pity.

Fortunately she wasn't listening. She was telling me how she had got to the commarde. I liked that, I didn't mind listening at all.

Meanwhile I ate pancakes with small square pieces of bacon baked in them and drank more orange juice from the jar which Edgar kept lugging about.

The girl asked me if I had ever taken LSD. I had to admit that I had not. Perhaps I should have but the occasion had never presented itself. The hippies who worked in our factory during the summer had often recommended the drug and had tried to tell me about its effects. I hadn't understood them. They told me about transparent trees, sound-visions and journeys in the subconscious. One hippie, a square-headed Englishman with an enormous beard had said that everybody should have the LSD experience at least once. But it seemed that I would miss this variety of adventure. I might try the drug if a reliable guide would offer to go with me. The hippies didn't inspire much confidence.

So I told the girl that I had never taken it.

"I have," the girl said.

I waited but she didn't continue.

"So?" I asked politely.

She showed me her wrists. Both showed the same wide scar. It hadn't been a razor.

"A breadknife?" I asked.

"A bayonet," the girl said. "My brother's. It's Chinese, he brought it back from Vietnam. I stole it off him and sharpened it. I used to keep it under my pillow. I didn't really have enough courage to use it."

"Did you have to do it?" I asked stupidly.

"Yes," the girl said, "and I *did* do it."

I looked at the scars again. The left was wider than the right. Obviously she was righthanded.

"I did it during a weekend. I was supposed to be alone but somebody happened to come along. I woke up in a hospital."

Her glass was empty and I gave her some of mine.

"And then you came here?"

"Half a year later. They put me in an asylum for a while."

Some adventure, I thought.

A moon-faced Buddha. An image of peace and power. For one week she sat opposite me and I never saw her move or shift.

Rupert had joined us.

"Do you have scars as well?" I asked.

"Not on my wrists."

I drank a little more orange juice.

"You don't come here if you don't have any scars," Rupert said. "You have to be desperate to start looking for the way out. Buddhism isn't for the satisfied."

"Buddhism," the girl said. "Buddhism doesn't interest me at all. I had a Christian education but Christianity doesn't interest me either. They are all words. Clubs you can belong to. At the university I was a club member. It was so terrible that I had to hack through my veins with a bayonet."

She pushed me with her elbow.

"Do you know what I am talking about?"

"I think so," I said.

"Well, tell him then."

"Rupert," I said. "I think I know what this girl is talking about."

"Good for you," Rupert said.

He knocked on the pockets of my jacket and found my tin of cigars. I lit his cigar for him. Rupert wove it under my nose.

"So what are you and this girl talking about?"

The girl put her hand on my arm.

"Buddhism is nonsense," I said. "If we are here to practice Buddhism we may as well give it up now."

"I know what I *shouldn't* do now," Rupert said. "Now tell me what I should do."

"You know damn well," the girl said.

And, very likely, he did.

I wandered away. I felt contented. The week was over. This was a party. I felt very detached from what might be bothering me. A temporarily incarnated spirit on a small ball in immeasurable space. A spirit without a soul. A spirit without a soul has nothing to lose.

My stroll through the room took me close to Peter who was sitting by himself in a corner. Edgar had just filled his glass again. He smiled at me and I smiled back.

"Are you ready?" asked Peter.

I was too relaxed to suspect anything.

"Sure," I said. "Ready for what?"
He shook his head.

Once again you are trapped.

For the umpteenth time you find yourself on the floor.
Defenseless.

This game defeats you at every corner.

But you go on trying it.

You scramble to your feet.

Perhaps the moment will come when you can no longer be
trapped.

It would be nice.

But it will take a long time, much effort.

It's a far moment, far in space, far in time.

Meanwhile you continue to fall over. And to get up.

And while you can, you proceed.

Eleven

Mount Meru

The orange juice stream hadn't dried up yet. I sneaked into the kitchen to see where it all came from. Edgar was pouring vodka into his jar. He looked a trifle guilty.

I saw a case full of vodka bottles and several four-gallon jars of orange juice.

"Don't worry," Edgar said.

"I am not worrying."

"Then help me with the ice cubes."

"What's this," I asked, "another exercise?"

"Maybe," Edgar said, and went on pouring.

"Maybe. Peter organizes these parties. Perhaps he wants to test us. Some of them in there are getting pretty tight. Listen."

I listened.

"They are talking loudly, do you notice?"

"Yes."

"And probably saying more than they should. Towards the end of these parties he attracts a circle around him. He eggs them on a bit, and they talk. They tell funny stories, about what happened during Rohatsu. How the jikki jumped at them. How they fell asleep. About visions they had. It all sounds funny when you are drinking vodka. But they were terrified in the Zendo at times. Were you terrified?"

"Give me a drink."

He poured some into my glass.

"You see," he said, "you drink and you talk about what happened in there and you relax."

"I haven't said anything."

He laughed.

"You don't have to."

I sipped my drink and Edgar went back into the room. It was time to go home. I had had enough.

I found Rupert in the cabin, fast asleep in his bag. The zip was closed up to the last notch. I opened it a little to give him air. One fierce eye looked at me.

"Go away," Rupert said, but then he changed his mind and sat up.

"Did you have a lot to drink?"

"So, so," I said.

"Hmm. You are not slurring your words. You must be reasonably sober. I was getting drunk so I left. A pity, I was enjoying myself."

"So why didn't you stay?"

"The master was there," Rupert said, "and I don't want to make a fool of myself, not if I can help it. He caught me once as it was."

"Did he say something to you?" I asked curiously.

"Nothing to do with you," Rupert said and then, after a while, giggled.

"Did he say something funny to you?" I repeated.

"No. He caught me. It isn't funny to be caught. I was laughing about something else. Shall I tell you?"

I was surprised, it wasn't like Rupert to tell me anything. Perhaps the liquor had softened him up or perhaps he was pleased that he wasn't the jikki anymore.

"O.K.," Rupert said, "give me a cigarette and I will tell you. And make some tea."

When we had settled down he giggled again.

"You don't know the people here so you don't know what goes on. I'll have to explain it all to you. You have seen the elderly guy with the bald head?"

"The one who twisted his ankle?"

"Yes. He is very tough, very stubborn I should say. He is, or was, an Orthodox Jew and he is set in his ways. He is a great believer in doing things properly. He built himself a very neat cabin and when he was all organized Peter sent him a lodger, a young hippie who wandered up about a year ago and who never left again. He is very bright, very quick, and very disorderly."

I laughed.

"Right," Rupert said, "that's why Peter shoved him into the old fellow's house. To shake him."

"And they get on."

"The hippie gets on with anyone. He doesn't care you see. He really doesn't care. He even sits well because he doesn't care. Pain doesn't seem to matter to him. He works on the farm, he does anything Peter tells him to do. He probably works hard on his *koans*. And if the old chap snaps at him he grins. He won't irritate the old chap on purpose but he can't help irritating him all the time."

"And he doesn't care about that?" I asked.

"Not at all."

"Go on."

"Don't rush me," Rupert said. "I am not good at telling stories. But this is what happened just now. Peter encouraged us to talk and he kept on looking at the hippie so eventually the hippie spoke up. He was telling us about the time he was having with the old guy during Rohatsu. The hippie would spend the intervals in the cabin talking and laughing and the old guy objected."

"He was right," I said.

"Sure he was right. And the hippie gave in. He shut up. But something bothered him. Some of the girls had to work in the kitchen a couple of hours a day, to help Peter prepare food for us all. They were given time off and wouldn't have to sit for a few periods. But when the hippie walked past the kitchen, and he did that a number of times a day, he always heard one girl snipping."

"Snipping?"

"Yeah, snipping. You know, cutting with a pair of scissors. Of course the hippie knew he wasn't supposed to break his concentration but this snipping got on his nerves. She was doing it all the time it seemed, every day, every time he walked past the kitchen. So one day he jumped up as he walked past the window and looked."

"Yes?"

"And he saw she was cutting some purple-looking fruit."

"Fruit?"

"Yes, and it is in the middle of winter. So he thought about it and didn't know what kind of fruit it could be and when he got home during the interval and sat there quietly in the old guy's cabin he started talking about it and asked the old guy what the girl could be snipping."

"Ha," I said.

"And the old guy got very cross. Rohatsu is a meditation week and meditation weeks are called *sesshins* in the training. So the old guy asked the hippie if he knew what '*sesshin*' means. And the hippie said 'Sure, *sesshin* means concentration of the mind.' "

" 'Fine,' the old man said, 'so shut up about your snipping. I don't want to hear. I want to concentrate.' "

I laughed politely, I thought the story was over.

"No, no," Rupert said, "wait! So now the old guy gets interested in the snipping. He had heard it too, we all heard it, but there are a lot of funny sounds around here and we didn't think about it. Only the hippie worried, and the old guy started worrying as well and began to mumble about the snipping and one day the old guy says he thinks the girl is snipping small eggplants for eggplants are the only purple fruits he knows, and the hippie laughs for there are no eggplants in this part of the world and certainly not in mid-winter. And then, on the last day of Rohatsu the old man comes tearing into the cabin, it's interval time again, and the hippie has got there first and is making coffee. 'Hey,' the old guy shouts, 'I know what it is. It's FIGS. She is cutting FIGS. They put little bits of fig in the cake we get for sweets everyday. FIGS.' "

I laughed and Rupert laughed and we finished up rolling around and holding on to our stomachs. I got cramps.

"O.K.," Rupert said, wiping his eyes. "Let's get some sleep. I have to get rid of all this alcohol."

"Is that how he twisted his ankle?" I asked before falling asleep. "Tearing about the cabin shouting FIGS?"

"No," Rupert's voice said from within the sleeping bag, "that happened later. He slipped on his way to the Zendo, we should sprinkle ashes on all that ice, I'll do it today."

I woke up because someone was shaking me. I was far away, talking to some Chinese monks I had met in my dream and they were hinting at the answer of my *koan*, smiling and making gestures which would have some meaning. Rupert was in the dream as well and my mother was snipping figs. I didn't want to wake up. It was a funny dream and I felt at home in it.

"Hey." It was Peter's voice.

"Yes?"

He was sitting on his haunches next to my head.

"I'll come back in an hour, I want you to go out with me. Or rather, you come to me. I'll wait for you in the car, it'll be parked in front of my house."

"Where are we going to?"

"You'll see. Put on a shirt and a tie and wash. You need a shave as well."

"Sure, sure."

He waved and was gone.

Rupert was sitting near the stove reading his notebook.

"Special treatment, hey?"

"Doesn't he take you out at times?" I asked.

Rupert smiled. "Often. Don't worry. I am not jealous. But there's a lot of jealousy around here. Everybody wants to be the favorite disciple."

I got up and began looking for my clothes and shaving gear.

"Have you ever been the favorite disciple?"

"Yes," Rupert said, "he spent a lot of time on me a year ago or so. I practically became his personal attendant, he took me everywhere. I even had to give him a massage in the evenings."

"Personal attendant to the Zen master," I said, knotting my tie.

"Sure. Very intense training that is. Too intense. When he stopped the treatment it took a while before I had digested it all."

"Did he drop you abruptly?"

"Yes," Rupert said, "one day he stopped. Someone else was selected. But he still takes me out now and then. We go shopping or he finds somebody who'll buy us a good meal in an expensive restaurant or we go for a long drive."

I made it just in time. Peter was in his car drumming his fingers on the wheel.

For ten minutes the car followed the coastal road, at every curve I saw a new bay or a little cape jutting out into the grey stormy sea. Perhaps one day I would have the chance to buy a boat and sail it from one of these bays, all the way to Holland and back again. I told Peter about the idea.

"I'll do it when I am old. It'll be better than sitting in a home for the old-aged in Amsterdam, I can always slip overboard when I get ill. It will be a nice death."

"How old?" Peter asked.

"Eighty."

He didn't comment.

"You can come with me. You'll be eighty-five," I said.

He grunted pleasantly. The idea probably appealed to him. He liked travelling, perhaps he felt cooped up here, surrounded by his disciples in a forest.

This had been Indian country once. The sun was low and lit up the rocks around us. The Indians were gone and now there was nobody around. We saw some cabins and houses, some of the houses were very big, mansions would be a better word, but they were all locked up.

"Vacation houses," Peter said. "We have some people here in summertime but not too many, they prefer to go south."

He obviously didn't feel like talking and we drove on in silence. After a while I asked where we were going. He didn't answer and I touched his arm. "Where are we going Peter?"

He turned round and looked at me as if he didn't know who I was.

"What, what?"

I asked again.

He grumbled to himself. "They want to know everything. Where are we going? Where are we coming from? That way you can keep on asking all your life."

I shrugged my shoulders and looked at the view.

A little later he did answer after all.

"We are going to see some friends of mine. A retired antique dealer, very rich. He lives here with his wife."

He pointed at a large bungalow on a hilltop and turned onto a dirt road. Three cars were parked in the driveway. The veranda was lit by ornamental lamps and the host, a handsome old man with thick white hair combed over his ears, welcomed us.

Peter introduced us. The hostess was waiting for us in the corridor and took us to the living room. She was younger than her husband and well dressed in a velour robe which reached the floor. I thought I had seen the dress before, in an expensive magazine. The article which went with the photographs was headed "The Careless Fashion."

I mumbled polite sentences. I shook hands. A gentleman with short gray curly hair was presented as a writer. The hostess had heard that I was a writer as well. Two writers shake hands. What a coincidence. Another gentleman made films. An artist as well. Another coincidence. I was given a martini and a small cigar. Courtesies dispensed with, the guests returned to their conversation and I looked around. I saw a display of framed photographs on the grand piano. They all featured our host. In some photographs he was accompanied by famous people. I recognized a queen, a film star and a composer.

I was given another martini and took it over to the bookcase. I studied the paintings, the furniture and the rugs. The house had been well placed, the bay windows displayed a magnificent view of the coast.

The guests drew me into their conversation, a pleasant conversation, friendly and on the surface of harmless subjects. Someone asked me why I was in America.

"I am visiting my friend Peter." I pointed at Peter.

The gentleman who had asked the question looked at Peter. "Yes yes," he said thoughtfully, "your friend is a Zen master I believe?"

I nodded.

"And you are also a Zen Buddhist?"

"Yes." Why not? If I have to be something I'll be a Zen Buddhist.

I was glad Peter wasn't listening in. Like the old teacher he never mentioned the word. There were a lot of words he didn't use. I had only heard him curse once, in Japan when a lady journalist, an American, had phoned him for the third time on one day to try and make an appointment for an interview. "Shit," he said and hung up, but the first two times he had been polite.

The gentleman, he was the writer I had been introduced to, looked at my martini and my cigar but said nothing.

Dinner was ready, the table had been beautifully set. The meal was delicious and the wine excellent. I sat next to the hostess near the kitchen which formed part of the room. She had no servants, I helped her to serve the guests. I filled dishes, poured wine and tried to divine what the guests wanted so that they wouldn't have to ask. It's a trick Chinese ship's stewards are very good at. But not being a Chinese steward and new at the game I blundered a few times.

I helped wash up.

"Very sweet of you," the hostess said.

"I am sweet," I said.

"Where did you learn to be so helpful?"

"Peter," I said, "Peter taught me."

I didn't quite understand what we were doing there. The conversation continued after dinner. We sipped brandy and said the right thing. I thought I knew Peter well enough to know that he didn't believe in polite conversation but there he was merrily prattling about why he preferred a VW to other makes of small cars, about the connection between this state and New York and about the small bugs which were such a menace during summer and what one could do about them (almost nothing). A guest enquired after the health of a mutual acquaintance; apparently someone had visited him recently.

"He is still very ill."

"What's the matter with him?" Peter asked.

"A disease of the skin. His skin becomes scaly, like a fish, something to do with old age. It's very painful and itchy."

The hostess shook her head. She had draped herself on a settee and made a charming picture, the color of her dress contrasted beautifully with the upholstery of the couch.

"Terrible," she said, "what a way to get to the end of it. That man is over eighty, he has to die anyway, and now he has to put up with a painful itch as well."

Her husband coughed, the subject wasn't very pleasant. A silence came and I thought I might as well say something.

"That man dies with an itch," I said, "half the population of this earth hasn't got enough to eat. The largest industry we know is the manufacture of arms and ammunition. One percent of the people of the United States is alcoholic or addicted to drugs. In Europe the percentage is lower but catching up fast. In South America prophylactics are illegal yet the population increases so fast that hunger becomes more of a problem by the day."

The host coughed again. He was right. But meanwhile an old man was suffering from a painful itch and had to take pills, pills to sleep, pills to calm his nerves, pills to fight the endless irritation of merely staying alive.

"This is the wrong planet," the hostess said. "Whatever you try to do here is hopeless. An individual may escape from suffering but the others will continue to feel pain, in one form or another. Perhaps the successful suffer more than the others, to see the others suffer is a subtle pain, but subtle pains can be very effective."

She looked at Peter. "You are a Buddhist aren't you?" she asked.

Peter didn't answer.

"I don't know much about Buddhism," the hostess said, "but the thought that we have more than one life comforts me. Perhaps we may earn the right to live on another planet one day. Perhaps there are planets without pain, where we can think and create and enjoy ourselves without any penance. The universe is so vast, there must be better places than this cursed little ball. I do think that I have deserved my life here and that it is silly to complain because I wouldn't be here if I didn't *have* to be here but there is sense in believing that there will be an end to this type of life, there must be a better way."

Everybody looked at Peter. He was innocently stirring his coffee.

"What do *you* think about it?" the writer asked.

"Why go so far?" Peter said. "Why wouldn't there be a satisfactory way of life here on Earth?"

"Aha," I thought, "he is going to talk about the Here and Now. Only Here and Now we can do something, if we do our best, and stay awake and know where we are and what we are trying to do."

"Somewhere in the Himalayas," Peter said, "there is a high mountain called Meru. The mountain is hard to find and the explorers walk past it. There is a lot of fog in that part of the highlands and it seems as if the inhabitants of the mountain are protected by nature from interference. But the mountain does exist, and there are people living on it. Very strange people. They are human, and they have bodies like we have but their bodies are perfectly shaped. They grow up very quickly and become adults but their bodies never seem to grow older than twenty-five, thirty years old maybe. The women are very attractive and the men are all athletes, with long legs and wide chests and narrow hips. They don't have to work. The mountain is covered with fruit trees and bushes providing berries and nuts. They have no urge to eat meat and never cook their food and they drink straight from the clear streams."

I studied the faces of the people in the room. Everybody seemed fascinated by Peter's low, almost hypnotic voice.

"But the most beautiful thing about these people is that they can fly. They have large strong wings consisting of light elastic bones and very thin supple skinwebs. Just a slight jump and they are airborne, gliding away; if they apply any strength at all they soar."

"Oh, how marvelous," the hostess said. She jumped off the settee, spread her arms, and danced lightly through the room. "You are describing it so well. I feel that I am on the mountain already. And that will be our future? Can we become like that, do you think?"

"But of course," Peter said. "From insect to animal, from animal to human, from human to angel. Why not? The circle continues, endlessly, we are always born again, and always in a different form."

The writer with the short gray hair had been listening attentively.

"What is the lifespan of these angels?" he asked. Peter smiled. "Exactly four hundred and ninety years. Then they die. And three years before they die they lose the power to glide and soar. Their life is long and old age approaches very slowly but one day they jump and fall back. The web between their wingbones has begun to rot."

I laughed. The hostess looked at me. The polite behavior of the evening had, for the moment, been forgotten. I saw the frightened face of a woman who is no longer young, whose beauty diminishes by the day, a woman who has seen the first signs of her death. The wrinkles, the first pair of spectacles, the small spots, so aptly named gravespots in English, have appeared on her hands. She is suffering from rheumatism.

"Do you think that's funny?" she asked. "Those angels lose their wings. Do you think that's funny?"

"No, madam," I said. "I don't think it's funny."

"So why do you laugh?"

I knew no answer. The writer helped me out.

"Our friend laughs because everything is relative. An angel will also come to the end of his life. The gods will die. The universe will dissolve one day. Whatever begins ends."

He looked at me. "Not so?"

I nodded, much relieved. I hadn't really meant to annoy the hostess.

"And isn't it true that the Buddha indicates a way to cut the circle? To break away from time? And from space?"

He was addressing Peter now.

Peter had got up. He was thanking host and hostess for their invitation and charming evening. We were helped into our coats and scarves. Within a few minutes we were back in the car.

"Here you are, pal," Peter said when he dropped me off at the road leading to Rupert's house. "Sleep well for maybe we'll have some work to do tomorrow. The next *sesshin* is still a few days off and we have to use our time."

He hadn't said a word during the long drive back from the antique dealer's bungalow.

I wasn't sleepy and I watched the taillights of his car fade away amongst the trees.

"Hello," a voice said and I jumped.

The voice laughed and I recognized the man who had suddenly detached himself from the bushes nearby. A tall man whom I had seen in the Zendo.

"I am out for a walk," he said, "if you aren't planning to go to sleep you can come and have a drink with me. I live in the next cabin. You have been using my water, I believe."

I had just made up my mind to go to bed but changed my plans. I had been wanting to meet this man, the mysterious neighbor who had always managed to be out when I lugged Rupert's buckets into his kitchen.

"Sure," I said and shook hands. The man introduced himself as Simon, the surname I didn't catch but it sounded Jewish. He looked like one of the tough young Jews I had met in Israel, the soldiers inseparable from their short machine guns and as much at home in the cities as in the desert. "Are you an Israeli?" I asked.

"No. But I might have been. I spent a few years out there but couldn't settle down."

"Are there any Arabs here?" I asked suddenly.

He laughed uproariously and slapped me on the shoulder.

"There is one, as a matter of fact. His parents are from Syria."

Within a few minutes he had a fire going in his grate. I settled down near the burning logs and he brought me some embroidered cushions. "Take it easy," he said, "lie down. Stretch out. We have sat up straight so much that we have forgotten the other side of life. Life in this cabin can be very pleasant if I have the time to enjoy it. Have some of this."

He poured me a glass full of brown liquid. It was a sweet brandy. I didn't like the taste but the drink was so strong that the taste didn't seem to matter.

I found it hard to follow Simon's rambling conversation. He bit off the words and used expressions I had never heard of but I managed to follow the general trend of what he was saying. He had been a dockworker and he still was, at times, when he ran out of money. He seemed to have been everywhere. In India. In Persia. In Ceylon.

"As a dockworker?"

Not as a dockworker. He filled my glass again. Ginger brandy, homemade by his parents on a small farm thousands of miles away.

He had travelled to these countries to find a guru.

"Did you find one?"

"You find what you are looking for," Simon said, "but I never really defined what I was looking for."

"But what did you find?"

"I found Swami-ji. A big strong square looking fellow with a bald pate. He was holy. Everybody said he was holy, that's why he was called Swami-ji, you follow?"

"And what did this big strong fellow do?"

Simon laughed.

"What didn't he do?"

I felt very comfortable, with my back against a brick wall, nicely warmed by the fire. He had put on some music and I was listening to a slow blues, carefully squeezed from the muted trumpet of a black musician and backed up by a whispered rustling and an occasional dry knock on a small drum.

"We should have some girls dancing here," I said.

"I didn't know you were coming," Simon said, "there are plenty of girls around and some of them dance very well. They are probably over at a party somewhere now. We have had some good parties here, pretty wild even, but I didn't feel like it tonight."

"Yes," I said. Perhaps I shouldn't have made my remark. I didn't mean a wild party. I had been thinking of a dance, slow graceful movement, with the trumpet and drums holding the dancers in their spell. An endless dance and I could have sat near the fire and watched it. But there was no need to explain what I felt. I wanted to hear about Swami-ji. Simon's face had changed. He had relaxed and looked kind and older, mature. He was using words I could understand now.

"What didn't he do? I met him in a narrow street. He was sitting in a small restaurant and looked at me and drew me towards him. He had some magic power, he could influence people very easily. It sounded just like the stories you read, the master draws his disciple towards him. I felt very pleased. I had found him. And it was the right place too. We met in a city near the Ganges, on very holy ground."

"And was he a master?"

"Well," Simon said and stirred the fire, "he certainly behaved like a master. Every Sunday he received in style. Old ladies would come to see him, and middle-aged ladies. Very wealthy ladies sometimes. They brought him gifts and money and tittered. 'Swami-ji. Swami-ji.' The great prophet receiving the enlightened. Very honorable. He knew how to impress people, especially women. And then we would go to the hospitals. I accompanied him wherever he went, carrying his bags. I was his first disciple."

I could imagine it. Simon would have been an impressive disciple with his short black beard and straight military bearing. "What did you do in the hospitals?"

"Visited the poor patients. He gave them small bunches of flowers. I had to make them for him. I even picked the flowers. It took me days and days to prepare for such a visit. I had to do everything he told me to do. If I was obedient I would become holy as well."

He interrupted his story and suddenly looked fierce.

"Marvelous, isn't it? But I did it. I picked flowers and I made lovely little bouquets. Thousands of them. And *he* would hand them around. He also cheered the patients up. Whenever he saw one of these very ill people, some of them so close to death that you could see them slipping away, he would march up to them, slap them on the shoulders and shout 'BE HAPPY!' He had a terrific voice. When he shouted the sick stopped wailing. He really frightened them. But when we left they were wailing again. There are no drugs for the poor in India."

"And what else would he do?"

"He drove a car. One of these funny little cars they make in India. He drove as fast as he could and he would blow his horn and shout a lot. He was the worst driver I have ever met but the police never bothered him. He was a holy man."

"Hmm," I said.

"Sure," Simon said, "I should have seen it straightaway, but it took me a long time. I wanted him to be holy you see? But one day he hit me in the face and I punched him in the stomach. I knocked him clean down and left him when he hit the floor. I didn't even look round. I had put a lot of weight behind that punch."

I didn't say anything. One shouldn't hit holy men. It's an unwritten law. If you hit holy men your hands will grow above your grave.

"So?"

"I went back to the States and became a dockworker again. It's interesting work. I used to drive a tractor pulling a lot of small cars and I got very good at racing about without ever running into anything. It's an art. And half the time we were on strike and I could wander round New York. I went to all the lectures. I don't think there is a single Hindu, Yoga, Sufi, Buddhist, Theosophist or whatever other crackpot faith expounder I haven't heard."

"Hey," I said, "this is a Buddhist settlement."

"So what. The people who talk about it are crackpots. I don't want to insult anybody. If they are honest they will admit it."

"O.K.," I said, "go on."

"So I got here. I found the address in a bookshop. Some people were discussing various types of training and they mentioned this place. I had saved some money and I could stay for a while. I have been here off and on for years. When I leave Peter gives the cabin to somebody else. They move out when I come back, or they stay if there is nowhere else for them to go. I can sleep in the loft if I have to."

"And is Peter the holy man you were looking for?"

He spat some brandy into the fire. I looked at the sudden flame.

"I am not looking for holy men any more."

"You have stopped the search altogether?"

"Search, search," Simon said. "I don't search. I am doing something, that's different. I walk, move one leg and then the other. I eat and I sleep. I help to build cabins. I milk the cows."

"And you meditate for some six hours a day."

"Yes," Simon said, "I meditate. It makes my legs hurt."

Twelve

An idiot

The settlement kept to the same timetable as the Zen monasteries in Japan. After the celebration of the Buddha's day of total insight there is a holiday partly filled by preparations for New Year. Around the fifth of January the routine of meditation and work is resumed and the monks go out again on their daily begging trips.

Peter had adapted the commarde. Begging was definitely out, American law wouldn't allow it and there was nowhere to beg anyway. Nobody lived within walking distance of the settlement and the disciples couldn't be expected to go begging in their cars.

Begging is an exercise in itself. I had often heard the old teacher speak about the "true spirit of begging." I hadn't understood what he meant but had supposed that he meant "dignity." The monks never stopped anyone. They walked holding their bowls. If anyone meant to give anything, the gift, either rice or money, was accepted with thanks. And if there was no gift, well, there was no gift. And the game of begging was a two-sided game. It involved both the giver and the receiver. Perhaps the master meant that to-give-and-to-receive is the perfect connection whereby the ego breaks and there is an end to all separation.

I missed the begging. In Japan I had never been allowed to go out with the monks but I had watched them every time they left the large gate.

But if there was no begging, there *were* holidays, another essential part of the training, and holidays may be celebrated. Consequently I didn't have a bad conscience when I woke up with a headache.

Peter was sitting near the stove. I greeted him but my voice croaked.

"Pardon?" Peter asked. I tried again. I sat up carefully and smacked my lips a few times. "I have a hangover," I said.

"How come? You weren't drunk when I left you on the track last night. Did you go to a party afterwards?"

"Not exactly a party," I said. "I ran into a man called Simon and I had some drinks with him."

"How many?"

"Five. It was ginger brandy. Bah."

"Why bah?"

"I don't like ginger brandy."

"So why did you drink it?"

"I don't know. It gave me a headache."

"And?"

"I'll fix it."

For a while I was very busy. I found aspirins and swallowed them, washed, went outside and rubbed my face with snow, stripped and rubbed my chest as well, went inside and made tea. It didn't take long.

I gave Peter a mug and sat down next to him.

"Good," Peter said. "Better than I expected. In Japan you would have refused to get up and I'd have had to drag you out of bed and push you into the bathroom. Remember?"

"Yes."

I didn't know whether he was right. That was ten years ago. The person I had been in Japan was very dead now. Change does not necessarily mean improvement. In a way I still admired the clochards of the large cities in western Europe. The down-and-outs who have completely stopped caring and who refuse to give their names because their names don't matter anymore. Nothing matters. They have even stopped suffering.

I could take him at his word of course. The word of a Zen master. But I would never do that, not even if I wanted to. Nobody else would either, none of the ones I had met anyway. This Zen master was blessed with very sincere disciples.

"What are your plans for today?"

I thought quickly. There were a lot of things I could do. I might help Simon the neighbor, he had a pile of wood to chop. I could go to the beach to have another look at the horseshoe crabs. There was a book in my suitcase I badly wanted to read. And it was just the sort of day to go for a long walk.

"I have no plans for today."

And I had promised myself to meditate. An hour at least.

"Good," Peter said. "Finish your tea and have a sandwich. You can take it with you and eat in the car. I want to drive the old truck around, there is some land which belongs to the estate which I have never seen. We need some good timber for the sawmill and I need some ground for potato fields. Put on a lot of clothes, it will be cold in the truck."

He meditated while I made the sandwiches and put on more clothes. He was the only person I knew who would do that, suddenly retract into deep concentration when his activity stopped. Not even the senior monks in Japan would meditate if there were others about, unless, of course, they were in the Zendo during a meditation exercise.

Would there ever be a time, I thought while I brushed my teeth, when meditation is an accepted general activity?

"Where is Father?"

"Father is meditating."

"Oh."

Father is meditating. He often does. The children meditate too when they have a chance. And Mother. And the neighbors. They are all disciples of the master of the neighborhood. There will be new classes, new ranks. When you want to be a member of the government you have to have solved a certain number of *koans*, otherwise your insight will not be sufficient to be able to help rule the country. The prime minister is a wise old fellow with a bald shaven head. He doesn't want anything. He has no possessions except what he needs for his daily simple routine. He is a high priest who nearly always wears the same clothes. The higher you go the simpler you become. Only the common people are rich, they still want to have property. The more impressive your residence the lower your place in society.

Perhaps the prime minister owns a mansion, but it is a gift from the people. He lives there to please his subjects but his bedroom will be a small bare room with white walls and his mattress will be thin and hard. He will get up at 3:00 a.m. and the ministers will visit him one by one for *sanzen*.

The state will be very rich. The bridges, roads, public buildings, airports, waterworks and national parks will be of the highest quality and well looked after. Nature will be nature again and full of wild life, but the wild animals will be tame.

I went outside. Peter followed me. The very old truck which I had seen on the farm was waiting for us on the track. Peter took the wheel and beckoned me into the passenger seat. He started the engine by twisting the ignition key.

"That's the first thing they'll do away with," I said.

"What?" Peter asked.

"Keys," I said. "Keys are quite unnecessary. A key is a symbol of fear. We need keys because we cannot trust each other. In Amsterdam I carry so many keys that I can't get them on one chain, I need two."

Peter looked surprised. "What of it?"

"It isn't right," I explained carefully and told him about the prime minister receiving his ministers at 3:30 a.m. every day.

Peter still looked surprised. Now I looked surprised as well. "But don't you think the future would have to be like that?"

"Daydreams," he said derisively. "Don't you have anything better to do?"

I felt the way my daughter probably feels when I try to educate her. Protest will get you nowhere but I wanted to try anyway.

"In that case Plato must have gone in for daydreams as well. In *The Republic* he describes the ideal state. The rulers are wise old men, tested in many different ways. They earn a penny a month and have little status. They rule, not because they want power, but because . . ."

"Because of what?"

I had to think. "Because of the exercise. They want to serve the people. They want to pass on their insight."

"Nonsense." He smiled at me.

"Plato was no idiot."

"No," Peter said, *"you* are an idiot."

We were driving through the forest. The little truck had trouble with the snow and the ice. Peter had the engine in its lowest gear but we made little progress. Every now and then the wheels began to spin and the truck slithered back. After half an hour of this we reached a fairly large plain.

"I have never been here," Peter said. "I wonder if my father knew this ground was here when he bought the estate. He has only been up here twice. He preferred the country back home."

"You want this land for farming?" I asked.

"Yes. I think it will be all right for potatoes. We have sufficient land for vegetables now but we could do with a good potato crop."

"A pity for all this beautiful land."

Peter shrugged his shoulders. "Plenty of land. You are in a very idealistic mood today. We live here and we need potatoes. We need a lot of food. And we need money as well. I can sell any surplus in town."

I had a vision of a large efficient farm. Tractors ripping up the ground with their large mechanical ploughs. Uniformed monks, very busy with their various tasks. Clerk-monks. A shop-monk. A balance sheet, compiled by an account-monk and his assistants. A computer digesting miles of plastic tape and indicating the best type of potato to be planted when and where. And if you have a computer you may as well use it. You can feed it sufficient data and it will tell you exactly what *koan* to use on what monk, and when.

"You want to run this place as efficiently as possible?" I asked.

"Why not?" Peter said. "If we do it we may as well do it properly. All these people here have to eat. Their children need to go to school. We need money. *You* work efficiently don't you? Surely you try to sell what you manufacture for the best price to the most reliable customer?"

"I try."

"Well?"

I looked unhappy.

Peter patted me on the shoulder. "Do your best and never mind the results. If things work out it's very nice. If, in spite of every-thing, they do not, it's very nice. Or the other way round. You might say that it's all wrong and not nice at all. Both conclusions are correct. You can laugh and you can cry, it doesn't matter at all what you do, but personally I would prefer to laugh. And mean-while we continue to do our best. For no reason at all. Don't attach a purpose to it. And go on till you die, or become too old. Then rest. You may get sick. You may have an accident. Or everything may work with you. You may be healthy and famous and rich right up to the last minute. Whatever happens is quite immaterial. No purpose."

"One may become insane," I said.

"Quite possible," Peter said pleasantly. "You do the best you can and then one day you are insane."

I still looked unhappy. Peter stopped the truck and switched the engine off. He asked for a cigarette and got comfortable in his seat.

"Before you came to Japan we had a young American in the monastery. He stayed two years. An intelligent boy, he had been at university when he developed some mental trouble. He wasn't really mad and he was released after a few months in an asylum. I can't remember what made him go to a Buddhist monastery, he must have had a good reason."

I was leaning with my back against the door and the lock slipped. I nearly fell out of the car but Peter grabbed me by the arm and pulled me back.

"That boy was very disturbed about having been a patient in a mental asylum. He wasn't convinced that they had cured him and he tried to talk to the old teacher about it. The master had no time for him. The boy was given *sanzen* and taught how to meditate and he had to fit in with the monastic routine and that was it. Then he tried to talk to me about his problem but the master told me spe-cifically not to listen to him. I was allowed to talk to him about the work he was supposed to do in the vegetable garden and the kitchen but I had to cut any conversation about his 'condition.' I thought it cruel at the time but I trusted the master."

I was leaning against the door again.

"Stop falling out of the car, it's hard to talk to you when you do that."

"And the boy became sane again?"

"I think so," Peter said. "But he was given excellent treatment. Every morning the master would walk around until he had found him. When he saw the boy he would say, 'Good morning. How are you? Are you a little crazy again this morning?' and then he would walk on before the boy had a chance to answer. The master always looked very kind when he spoke to the boy."

I could imagine it very easily. I knew the old master when he looked kind. A small thin man with a large head and piercing eyes. He had a trick of sending vibrations towards you, vibrations of love and power, or just love. I never knew the exact components of the vibrations. And whenever he did that you felt as if you could do anything you liked and lived in the best of all possible worlds. But the old teacher didn't make you drunk or high. He gave you a whiff of reality.

"And how is the boy now?"

Peter stared thoughtfully at the cluster of trees dead ahead. "I never saw him again after he left the temple. He left in peace. I think he went back to university, got his degree and got a job and married and had a family. Somebody told me about him, years later. He is all right now I guess. But something else may have happened to him by now."

"So he didn't continue the training."

Peter shook his head. "Watch it! Training this, training that. We are nothing special here. Some of you people talk as if we are a secret brotherhood with a magic shortcut. It's nothing like that. The training is anywhere."

"And the masters? They aren't anywhere."

Peter looked despondent. "When you have an idea nothing and nobody will ever break it. Masters aren't anywhere, but the teaching is."

"The Buddha's teaching?"

Peter gave up. He started the engine and we bounced our way through the landscape. Suddenly he stopped the truck. "Get out here a minute. There's a ditch a little further ahead. I don't think it's very deep. We may get through it if I can get this truck to work up a little speed. Just have a quick look."

I saw a vague dip and a shadow behind it. When I got close I could see that the ditch was quite deep. It would hold the truck and she would never be able to climb up the steep side by herself. It was a perfect trap, specially made to catch small trucks. I walked back and reported in detail.

"Never mind," Peter said, "it'll be all right. Hop in and hold on."

I held on, one hand against the roof to protect my skull. Perhaps I should have refused to drive with him but I was curious to see how it would end. Peter accelerated and hit the ditch at top speed. The truck's nose dived into the small precipice and we stopped halfway up the other side and slid back. The engine rattled, coughed and cut out.

Peter stared at me. The shock had knocked the air out of his lungs and he was rubbing his head. Fortunately he had been wearing a thick fur cap.

When I saw there was nothing wrong with him I giggled and when I saw an expression of vivid reproof gliding over his face I laughed outright. My door had been flung open by the impact and I fell out again and tumbled about in the snow, howling with laughter and pointing at Peter who slowly clambered out of the truck's cabin.

"Yes yes," he said. "It's OK. You were right. I should have believed you. Now you can help me get this vehicle back on the level again."

"We'll never do it," I said. "Impossible. We need an elephant or a tractor, a big tractor."

He still wouldn't believe me and tried to start the engine. He kept on trying till the battery was flat. I sat on a rock and patiently watched. Finally he gave up and we walked home. On the way he told me the names of the trees we passed. It seemed as if he had forgotten the truck.

We had lunch and returned with a tractor. The tractor didn't have enough power and we borrowed another one from the nearest farm. One of the disciples fixed the engine but it took a lot of time and trouble. Finally the truck started. We drove her back to the house and Peter discussed the future potato crop. The incident was closed.

Rupert was waiting for us at the house. Peter jumped when he saw Rupert's face.

"What's wrong?"

"Jeremy collapsed. It happened while you were out there. He has been feeling ill for some time now. Nobody knows what's the matter with him. We carried him to his house and put him in bed but he looks terrible."

Peter looked white in the face. "Did you phone the doctor?"

"We phoned for an ambulance as well. It should be on the way. One of the girls who is a nurse says he may be close to death."

"I'm going to see him," Peter said and jumped in his car. I went with him and he didn't stop me. "The boy has been ill for some time, it's true," he said in the car. "I told him to go to bed but he wanted to finish Rohatsu. He said he felt all right, just tired. But we were all tired."

Jeremy lived in a two-storey house, a few miles down the highway.

"What's this?" Peter asked as we drove up the track. A large tree had fallen right on the house. The roof was too high to determine the exact damage but the sight of that big tree leaning on the house wasn't pleasant. A young woman carrying a baby came out of the house. I didn't know her but I remembered Jeremy, a small man with a little beard who had been sitting with us. I hadn't noticed that he looked ill but I had, most likely, been too wrapped up in my own sufferings at the time.

"This isn't our day," the girl said. "Last night the tree fell on the house. The storm broke it, but it seems strange. The tree wasn't dead and it wasn't catching the wind. It just broke and hit us and we couldn't figure out what had happened. And then this morning the bank sent a very threatening letter about the repayments of our loan. And now Jeremy has suddenly collapsed." She was doing her best not to cry. Peter put his arm around her and kissed her on the cheek. He went into the house and I waited outside, with the woman and her child. I didn't say anything, there was nothing to say.

The ambulance arrived and a doctor. Within a few minutes Jeremy was in the car. To me he looked as if he was already dead. I couldn't see any movement in his pale face.

Peter went with the ambulance.

"I can't go," the girl said, "the baby has to be fed."

"It's all right," Peter said. "I'll go and I'll telephone to the store as soon as I can. One of the boys will wait in the store for my call and then he'll come and tell you. The doctor says he is in bad shape but we're just in time. They'll pull him through in the hospital. Don't worry."

The ambulance drove off, its light turning round and the doctor's car followed. Rupert had joined me.

"Would you do something for us?" the girl asked.

"Sure, sure," Rupert said. "What is it?"

"We are out of logs in the house and we need some. There are plenty in the cellar but I'm not strong enough to carry them all up."

I was glad of the opportunity to do something and we spent the next few hours carrying firewood, building a gigantic pile near the stove in the livingroom. The boy who had been waiting in the store came with Peter's message. Jeremy would be all right but he would have to stay in hospital for a while. His disease had been diagnosed as diabetes. His body had been eating up all its reserves and had, when there was nothing more, started to digest its own muscle tissue.

We were still carrying wood when Peter returned from the hospital. He had recovered and was radiating warmth and power. The girl relaxed and the baby laughed.

"We'll fix this tree for you," Peter said. "I'll just have a look at the roof."

We went outside. The tree was leaning on the house at a very steep angle.

"Ha," Peter said and walked straight up the tree, without even holding on to it. We saw him walking about on the roof and he came down again in the same way, almost running and jumping into the snow.

"Not much damage. I'll get a chainsaw and we'll cut it in half. The top half will slide down and we'll guide it with ropes so that it won't scratch your wall. And tomorrow we'll chop it up for firewood."

Some of the others came to help and the whole job was done within an hour. Peter stayed with the girl and cooked a meal, washing up afterwards. I helped and we walked back together.

"What about that bank loan?" I asked.

"It will be paid soon," Peter said. "They have had enough problems for a while. We mustn't overdo it."

"Did you arrange for that tree to fall on the house?" I asked.

"No," Peter said, "but I did drive that truck into the ditch. That was very silly of me."

Thirteen

A *koan* is a piece of tissue paper

It had been a very long day. Rupert's cabin was cold when I got to it. The ashes in the stove glowed and it took half an hour before the logs which I had put in caught fire. I made coffee, sat as close to the stove as I could and looked through my Rohatsu notes.

Rupert came home and yawned. "We must have a bath tomorrow. I'll ask Simon if he'll let us use his shower. There's a stench of old goat in here."

He looked at my notebook. "What are you reading?"

"My notes."

"On *koans?*"

I didn't answer. To discuss *koans* isn't proper procedure. He asked again and I grunted.

"Don't be so shy. I have a notebook as well. I suppose most of us have. Peter doesn't encourage it but it's reasonable that we try to keep a record. He probably did it himself when he trained in Japan."

"He did," I said. "I often saw him scribbling away."

Rupert yawned again and sat down. "It's quite useless, I suppose. These notes do nothing for you and all you achieve is that you have another possession to worry about. You may lose the book and all the enlightenment goes out of the window."

"*Koans* are pieces of tissue paper," I said.

Rupert had been unzipping his sleeping bag but now he looked up. "What's that?"

"Not my remark," I said. "The old teacher said that once. There was a monk in Kyoto who was always catching cold. He would blow his nose in paper handkerchiefs and keep them in his sleeve after he had used them. The head monk made a remark about it. He thought it was a filthy habit. The monk's sleeves were so full of paper that he rustled as he walked past."

"Go on," said Rupert, "I like to hear about the old master. So what happened?"

"The old master heard about it and used the paper handkerchiefs in his next *teisho*, the official Sunday lecture in the great *dharma* hall when all the outside disciples and laymen came to listen to him. He warned us not to hang on to the *koans* we had passed but to throw them away, as we throw away used pieces of tissue."

Rupert was looking at me as if he expected me to go on.

"There is no more," I said.

Rupert grinned.

"All right, all right."

He slid into his sleeping bag and turned out the light, leaving me to scramble for my blankets in pitch darkness.

Fourteen

The fox

I woke up. Rupert had gone and the alarm hadn't been set. It was close to 9:00 a.m., ridiculously late for life in the commarde. We were still in the holidays and I stretched luxuriously under the blankets. Coffee, breakfast, a cigarette, wash up and wander away. A day of emptiness.

There was a note on the table signed by Rupert. "Have gone for the day, enjoy yourself."

I would.

But within an hour I was at the farm, looking for Peter. I remembered the story the old teacher had told about a devil. A devil who has nothing to do, no routine or program, is liable to get himself and his master in dire trouble. I smiled at my own thought. Life at the commarde was pretty safe, I wouldn't be able to get into much trouble. But still, one never knows. I might as well watch it.

Emptiness, the core of Buddhism. Emptiness, the great goal which is to be reached by losing everything there is to lose. Emptiness, the great danger. If you have nothing to do, you run a lot of risks and the training frowns on you. Yet the final goal is to have nothing more to do, to be nameless, to be stripped of the last aggression, the last defense.

When Bodhidharma, the Indian Zen master who took Zen to China, was invited by the emperor, the meeting immediately became a display of vanity on the emperor's part. He told the master about the many monasteries and temples he, the emperor of China, the son of heaven, had originated and financed. He told Bodhidharma about the great spreading of Buddhism, all over China, and all due to him, the emperor. He asked the master what this important display meant and Bodhidharma said, "It means nothing, a great emptiness."

And when the emperor, stupefied, asked the master who he, this messenger giving this weird reply, really was, Bodhidharma said, "Don't know," turned on his heels and left the court.

I looked for Peter but was told he had left for the day. The farm was very quiet. I found a girl in the cowstalls and asked if I could help her.

"No," she said, looked at me and asked, "who are you anyway?"

"Don't know," I said, turned on my heels and left the cowstalls.

I wandered into the forest thinking about Bodhidharma, the free spirit who knew exactly what he was doing and where he was doing it. A free spirit creates the situations he chooses to be in. Where would the old monk have gone to after leaving the heavenly court of Peking? What would he have had for dinner that night and where would he have found the money to pay for it? Or was he beyond all that, like the advanced yogis who can live on the wind?

And where was I going now?

I had lost my way. The paths on the estate all looked like each other. Everywhere around the bare trees faced me, creaking, sometimes even exploding in the frost. Eventually I managed to find Rupert's cabin and ate. I spent the afternoon meditating, timing myself with the alarm clock, which I set for periods lasting a little under one hour. I gave myself ten minute breaks and did physical exercises to restore the bloodstream in my legs. I had often read about yogis sitting for six or more hours at a stretch but I had never seen anybody actually do it. I slept for an hour, read a bit and wandered out into the forest again. The sky was overcast filtering the moon and the snow reflected the vague mysterious glimmering light.

What was I doing in this world?

I didn't have to worry about making a living over here, there was nobody to care for. No daily work, no needs. No vacation either, no doctor had told me to relax for a while. I was suspended in my own existence, wandering in a world of bare trees. The trees were alive. I flashed my torch and could see the buds, waiting for spring.

I had lost my way again and I was quite alone. A free spirit creates the situations he chooses to be part of. The emptiness frightened me. Would I allow fear to creep close and jump me? Would I sit down on this dead log, smoke a cigarette and dream in circles? "No fear," I thought. I kept on walking. I moved one leg, then the other. The direction is probably right, in any case I know of no better direction. There is a *koan* to be solved. I have to blow my nose on it, clear my head, and then throw the *koan* away and blow my nose on a fresh *koan*. The master has an endless supply. They'll clear my head, all of them, and the final one may blow my head off.

I remembered one of Peter's *teishos*.

He had watched us kindly, us, the forty disciples huddled in his living room.

"What you are doing here isn't easy," he said. "Your body hurts and your mind creaks with stress. The trouble you are going to, and which you think will release you in the end, is nearly maximal."

I had expected him to say something pleasant after this appreciative preface, a few comforting words which would help us through the final part of Rohatsu.

"But," Peter said promptly, "you must be aware that it is quite possible that this training may not give you any result whatever."

And he had bowed to us, indicating that the lecture was over.

I had left the room at the same time as Edgar. We had both been grinning, on our way to the Zendo where we had two hours of painful quietness waiting for us. It is amusing to experience a change. Any teacher, any trainer, any pedagogue who aims to get his pupil from point A to point B, will, from time to time, try to encourage.

But a Zen master does not encourage.

He may weaken, and encourage a beginner, stuck on his first *koan* and groping about in the dark and knocking his head against real or imagined obstacles. He may tell the stumbler that he, the master, has been faced with a first *koan* as well, long ago now, and that he remembers the time when he didn't even know where he could hang himself because there wasn't a beam left in the structures of his thinking which would support a feather.

But the encouragement is for the very first beginning. The master prefers to *dis*courage, to destroy the supports, to push the disciple to the point of no return where he has to make his leap and there is never any guarantee that he may land safely.

And when a master encourages, he encourages doubt. Whenever the disciple thinks that he is walking on firm ground the master shakes his head and rings his bell. Hakuin's rhinoceros of doubt, pointing at your forehead with his sharp double horn.

And there are no shortcuts.

In Japan I had been friendly with a lay disciple of the old teacher, a dentist who had paid me the rare compliment of criticizing my behavior. I had been riding my scooter dressed in what I had thought to be a neat summer kimono and he had stopped me and told me to go back and change. What I was wearing was some sort of undergarment, which can only be worn indoors. He had probably felt bad about this direct approach and invited me to come and have tea with him and I had used the opportunity to ask him why he had chosen this particular training. There are many paths in the Buddhist teaching, he might have chosen another, easier, method.

"I thought Zen to be a shortcut," the dentist said.

"Isn't it?" I asked.

"There are no shortcuts," he said, and changed the subject.

No shortcuts and no simplicity. Only one part of the teaching is simple. The disciple has to meditate. For hours and hours. Every day. Insight is caused by long sitting. Early in the morning when the world isn't moving yet. Quietly, in a corner of the room. Or in a meditation hall, or outside, on a rock under a tree, or in the loft of an old gable-house in Amsterdam, or a proper temple with mats on the floor and special cushions and perhaps a Buddha statue on a shelf. The quiet vibrations of smoldering incense can be helpful. But meditation can be done anywhere. There are people who meditate under the bridge of Calcutta where the traffic grinds continuously. Meditation is the Zen master's recipe, the base of his teaching. And for the rest he forces you to do the impossible and make you jump through walls or off the precipice. Let go! Let go! Don't hold on to anything. And don't disregard your doubts. Let your doubts move you on. Don't think that you have found something because it's about time that you have found something. Go on, do the best you can. And know that there is no guarantee whatever that you will ever make it.

I was mumbling to myself as I walked. All very well, but here I was in the forest, alone, lost and not too sure about what I was trying to do. By allowing myself to wander about in emptiness I was taking a grave risk. The old teacher was right when he warned about living without a routine. I might have been better off if I had stayed in the cabin, meditating or reading near the fire. Here doubt attacked me with its full force.

I wanted to meet someone. But who?

A human being? Another lost soul? But what good would that do?

Not a human being.

What then? An angel, a Bodhisattva? An illuminated being from a higher sphere?

No, no god. He would make me jealous.

The fox approaches you gracefully. His plumed tail points at the sky. He is a large fox, about twice as big as the little foxes you have seen in the Dutch zoos or the stuffed corpse you were shown in the room of the biology teacher at high school.

This is a very beautiful fox, with a gleaming reddish-brown back and a fluffy white belly. He is dancing on the snow, lifting his feet with no effort at all. He is coming straight at you.

Good God, you think, there are still miracles in the world. A being which has nothing to do with me, a human. An animal who lives in the forest, who knows every sound, every form, around here.

He is large and healthy and intelligent. He has enough to eat and all his meals are adventures.

The fox is still coming at you. You have stopped thinking, you are merely meeting a fox. You wouldn't even have been frightened if, on this narrow track lined with moonlit trees and protected by the night's silence, you had met a wolf, or a bear.

The fox doesn't slow down. He comes so close that you can look him in his large light-brown eyes. He is looking at you as well and he jumps, not at your throat, but aside, off the track, and there is no change in the rhythm of his movement.

You look back and he is on the path again, his plumed tail waving up and down. You keep looking at him till he disappears in a bend of the path.

Rupert was staring at me when I got back to the cabin. He probably felt responsible for my comings and goings but I didn't give him a chance to open his mouth.

"I have seen a fox, Rupert," and I indicated how big the fox had been. "With a plumed tail and light-brown eyes."

He allowed me to finish my description and poured hot water on the powder coffee.

"A good omen," he said when I had finally finished. "I have never seen him but I have heard stories about him. He must be the same fox. There are so many of us living around here now that the wild animals have gone away but that fox keeps on showing himself. He isn't afraid of us."

I thought of the ghost stories of Japan, often dealing with foxes who may be witches or dead disciples of masters. The witches can take on the form of a fox at will while they leave their own human body in a safe place but the dead disciples take the fox's form as a kind of punishment. They have committed some sin, some error, and a fox's life is their fate.

I was sure that this fox was neither a witch nor a temporarily punished human soul. He was a fox in his own right and he enjoyed being a fox. And he had helped me considerably, appearing at exactly the right moment.

"I have news for you," Rupert said as he gave me my coffee.

"Tonight we can only sleep for four hours. We'll have to get up at 2:30. Peter has cancelled the rest of the holiday, tomorrow we have a new *sesshin* waiting for us. I have been driving around all evening to tell everyone."

"And what did they think about it?" I asked sleepily.

"Ah well," Rupert said, "they grumbled a bit but I don't think anybody really minded. We came here to do something, not to visit each other and drink ginger brandy."

I let it go. I saw the plumed tail of the fox and it swept me asleep. When the alarm's grinding woke me up I felt as if I had slept for at least eight hours and the fox had been with me right through the night.

Fifteen

Karma and whether or not to be a rabbit

The next *sesshin* had started and was slowly gliding away into the past. Peter had told us, when it began, that the *sesshin* was supposed to be a "little" one. I couldn't see anything "little" about it. Like any *sesshin* it would last seven days, and we were sitting some seven hours a day. We were working in the mornings, mostly chopping wood and stacking it, but there was a nice long break in the afternoon. That break had become my private adventure and I was, almost desperately, using the two hours of which it consisted.

I had discovered Simon's rock garden and, perhaps even more important, his private lavatory. The blue jays had taken me there. I saw them fussing about amongst the trees, talking to each other with their raucous voices and had taken some bread with me, trying to win their confidence. I meant to see if they would come and eat from my hand. But they kept flying away and, following them, I suddenly found myself in a very strange garden. The snow-covered bushes looked as if they had been planted and circled an area in which someone had placed a fairly large number of strangely shaped rocks. It was late in the afternoon when I found the garden and the rocks threw their shadows far across the thick snow. I didn't want to walk about too much as my tracks would spoil the almost austere geometrical designs of bushes, rocks and shadows. I sat on one of the rocks and merely gazed about me.

Now that I had stopped trying to make contact with the jays they no longer played their game of hide and seek and hopped around me until one, the female, landed on my arm with a soft thud and began to pick at the bread. She shoved the largest part of the sandwich off my hand and her mate picked it up and flew to another rock where he began to eat it slowly. The silence calmed him and eased his greed. I felt very peaceful and lit a cigarette. The place was all mine, or ours rather as the jays were now my friends, and I could do with it as I pleased.

I began to compare the garden to other gardens I had seen, Japanese temple gardens and gardens of the large mansions in Holland where the merchants of the Golden Age once lived. The dreamlike quality of the rocks and their shadows on the snow reminded me of some of the paintings of Dali and Delvaux but then I got shocked back into reality. I was doing it all wrong. Why compare? Why, for the sake of all holy men, wizards and fakirs, why compare?

I should look at it, I told myself, just look at it. Become one with it, as the old teacher had told me in Kyoto. To compare is the activity of the poor man, the man who will always be poor because he keeps poverty in his mind. He tries to grab new possessions and wants to evaluate them by comparing them with other things he has grabbed before. This garden was one of the manifestations of reality, the miraculous world to which we all belong. Why want to own it if it belongs to us anyway? And who is this "me" and this "us"? The garden *is*. And if it is destroyed, by a bulldozer or an earthquake, or because the universe pulls itself inside out, as it may very well do, any minute now, the reality will still *be*.

So I sat on the rock, and tried to be for a while.

Until I heard the sound of a door opening and closing, followed by the sound of someone clearing his throat and followed by the sound of someone creaking through the snow. I didn't see anything but I could determine the place of the sounds and I went to investigate. There was a cluster of trees nearby and right in the middle of this cluster, on a bulge of ground in the shelter of an immense pine tree, a small cabin with a sloping roof and an ornamental door. I approached the cabin with some reverence. It might be a meditation hut or contain a private altar with a Buddha statue. The roof looked Japanese but the door was very American, I had seen doors like that in some of the more elegant holiday houses around, oak doors, thick, with elaborately carved garlands of flowers and leaves.

I opened the door carefully, ready to bow to the unfathomable smile on the face of the Buddha statue but stepped back and laughed. This was no place of reverence, it was a privy, plain and simple. A low seat with a hole, nothing else. And very convenient. I took my trousers down and sat on the seat. The door closed.

This wasn't so good. It was dark in the cabin, the small window hadn't been washed for some time and the pine needles outside absorbed most of the light of the low sun. I pushed the door open with my foot and propped a broom, found in the privy, against it so that it wouldn't fall closed again. And then a real wave of happiness surged through me. This was *it*, undoubtedly. There was no temptation to compare this time. The open door gave me a view of a narrow path, winding through the trees and the heavy dark-yellow light colored the dead needles covering the track and the branches of the trees with their shining bark. Whoever had built this privy in this particular place was an artist, a master architect of landscapes. Not even in Japan had I ever seen such blatant beauty. The sudden activity of my bowels coincided with the general explosion of awareness. "An enlightening shit," I thought and laughed and a voice hailed me.

"Is that you?" the voice questioned and I shouted back that it was me.

"Come and have tea when you are finished," Simon shouted. I reluctantly pulled up my trousers and bowed to the privy.

In the Kyoto monastery the privy had a miniature altar, high on a shelf, to remind the monks that the Buddha nature is everywhere and can be realized in the meanest actions. I hadn't been able to prove the thought at the time.

Simon was waiting for me at the end of the path and I apologized for having strayed into his garden and used his lavatory without his permission.

"That's all right," Simon said. "What's mine is yours. But the garden isn't mine and neither is the privy."

"But surely all this belongs to your grounds here?" I asked.

Simon smiled. "I suppose so," he said, "but I was only given this small piece of land right here by Peter. All the other ground is part of his estate."

"Did you design the rock garden and build the privy?"

"No," Simon said, "it was here when I came. A very odd man did all that. He was in Japan, I am told, for a number of years and spent all his time in wandering around Zen gardens."

"Didn't he study Zen as well?"

"Sure," Simon said, "he meditated and was a master's disciple, but the gardens were his life."

"And why did he leave here?"

Simon smiled again. "Why do people leave?"

I didn't insist. I knew why people left. I had left myself. You can leave on your own, and the master can tell you to go. "Will he come back?"

Simon looked in the direction of the rock garden. "I think so. That garden is perfect. Wherever he is now, he will think of it. He was here for quite a few years. I have been told that he is wandering around the country now, in a small camping truck, with his dog. He takes odd jobs and stays for a while and then he starts his truck and he is off again. Eventually he'll show up. He hasn't finished here and he should be coming back until, one day, the master tells him that there is no more."

"Will we have to be *told* that there is no more?" I asked.

Simon patted me on the head, they all seemed to have learned that trick from Peter.

"Don't ask so much," Simon said, "don't you know that all the answers are in yourself?"

"I know nothing," I said peevishly.

We had tea in his luxurious living room, with the fire spreading its crackling warmth. Simon was talking about *karma* and reincarnation.

"This reincarnation business was quite a comfort to me once," Simon said, "until I realized that reincarnation means the will to live. It is a power which drives us on, step by step, towards death, and death is a door. It says EXIT on one side, and you are forced through it and wander on and when you look back it says ENTRY, and when you go further, as you have to, there is no choice, there is another door coming near saying EXIT. It is the door of birth.

And so it goes on. There is no end to it. And you are always between doors, and suffering continues."

"You can laugh at times," I said, remembering my recent merriment in the privy.

"Sure," Simon said, "I shouldn't complain. But the idea of having to go on and on bores me. It's no comfort to know that one life follows another and is itself the prelude to a new life. Life continues and with it fear. Fear of death, fear of birth. Real, definite death would be more of a comfort. It will be a true ending. No more to come."

"All this trouble for nothing?" I asked.

"Nothing is the key," Simon said.

I jumped up. "It's time, we have to go back to the Zendo. If we go now we won't have to rush."

"All right," Simon said, following my example, "I hate rushing too. There's nothing worse than having to run up to the Zendo worrying all the way about whether you are going to make it on time or not."

Outside he slipped and fell against the wall of his cabin. A nail scratched his hand which began to bleed. I bandaged the wound for him.

"Do you always carry bandages with you?" he asked.

"Of course," I said and showed him my collection. A many purpose knife, a small pair of scissors, a torch, a screwdriver, sunglasses, notebook, ballpoint, cleaning gear for my glasses, etc.

"Very practical," Simon said.

"Aren't you practical?" I asked.

"About the same as you are," he said. "I carry a similar collection as yours, but no bandages. I'll buy some tomorrow. They will be handy. Sure I am practical. I work and try to earn enough to be able to live comfortably. In the meantime I try to learn. I believe in *karma*, I will have to be in a continuous position of being able to accept the consequences of my previous deeds. And I try to do the right thing when I can do it, which is about all the time."

"Yes," I said, "one has to be careful." The conversation frustrated me. "Certainly," I said, "we have to be practical. Only do what is necessary. Earning money is necessary for instance, but only up to a point. After that point money creates nothing but soap bubbles, power and property you can't use. My uncles own a lot of houses, yachts, stuff like that. The houses produce rent which they can't spend and the yachts rot in some harbor. To earn money that way is not very intelligent perhaps."

"Exactly," Simon said and patted me on the shoulder. He giggled. "It seems I am more intelligent than your uncles. To spend time here, here where earning money is almost impossible, is a pretty clever occupation. Like meditation and being guided by a master."

"Guided to where?" I asked.

Simon stopped and I stopped as well and looked back. He made a good picture with the pine trees framing him and the blue jays circling above his head. A squirrel had followed us and was watching us from a low branch, nervously holding on to a nut.

I walked back and asked again. "Guided where?"

"Look here," Simon said irritably, "how the hell would I know? Maybe *you* should know. Maybe you are an advanced disciple. I never even know who is advanced and who is not. But I do know that I have no real knowledge. Or are you trying to ask me one of these tricky questions to show how clever you are, or, why not, are you trying to help me on my way perhaps?"

It was my turn to giggle. It's the master's task to ask tricky questions. Disciples only stumble along and think they discover something or other every now and then.

"Don't worry, Simon," I said, "I am not trying to be clever. And I don't know where I am going. I suppose we should all be on our way to Nirvana but it seems to me, lately, that it would be unacceptably arrogant to assume that *we*, of all people on the planet, will reach, thanks to this training, a sphere *outside the circle of reincarnation*. Why us, and not the others?"

Simon had started walking again. "Well," he said, "I don't know what the others are doing. I am concerned with the training, I am a master's disciple. My *karma* took me to this forest and all these funny little buildings and here I meditate and meet my master. Here I can change my *karma. Karma* is real, I suppose, for even Peter mentions it occasionally although he evades all direct questions or answers them in such a way that you are still groping around for something you can put your hand on. You know the story about the boy who went to Mr Singh?"

"No," I said.

"Listen to this," Simon said and put a heavy hand on my shoulder. "There was a boy here who only stayed for a few months. A real mystic with an enormous black beard for hiding his face behind. He had decorated his head with gold earrings and he wore an embroidered suit. The rear of his jacket was most impressive. He had embroidered a mountain on it which was being climbed by dragons, evil forces. And on the top of the mountain throned a magnificent rooster, the symbol of Good. A very strange fellow he was, but quite likeable. He meditated a lot, far more hours than we did, and it took a good deal of effort to get him to do some work. Whenever we had to chop wood or work in the gardens I would have to go and fetch him and I even had to pull him out of the Zendo where he was sitting by himself. All he wanted to do was sit still and concentrate."

"Not bad," I said jealously.

"Some show, eh?" Simon asked. "I don't mind meditation but I don't really enjoy it. It is only because of the discipline that I meditate a lot, if I wasn't forced I would sit for an hour a day, but that boy sneaked into the Zendo whenever he could. And still, he didn't seem to be getting anywhere, or so he said. He claimed that he would sit there, reasonably quiet, with his thoughts pushed away and his stomach or central nerve knot or whatever it is we have around there, glowing away like blazes but nothing really happened to him. He wasn't getting enlightened he said."

"What did he expect?" I asked. "Fireworks? Visions?"

"Hmm," Simon said, "what is it we expect? I also ask myself at times what I am sitting for, it seems that the only thing happening is the jikki hitting his crazy bell every twenty-five minutes."

"So he left, this embroidered boy of yours?"

"He left," Simon said, "he didn't run away. He announced his departure and said he wanted to visit a guru in India, a very special guru who claimed that he could enlighten his disciples by merely touching their heads in a certain way. The man was supposed to be called Singh and the boy had the address. 'Singh' means lion and it is the surname of most Sikhs. There must be millions of Mr. Singhs in India, but the boy claimed he would find *his* Mr. Singh without any trouble at all and Peter let him go."

"He couldn't very well prevent him from going," I said. Simon nodded. "But Peter said something which interested me. He said that he wondered if Mr. Singh would be able to change that boy's *karma*."

I thought about it. *Karma* cannot be destroyed by Mr. Singh, that was pretty obvious. It seemed as if Peter was telling us that *karma* was hindering us, our own *karma*, the relentless result of our previous actions. And we might assume that Peter believed in *karma*, or he wouldn't have mentioned the word. And if he did believe in *karma* he would also believe in reincarnation for *karma* is the force which kills us and shoves us back into the world through our mothers' vaginas. Now bad *karma*, according to the rules, can be diminished, even broken, but only by our own effort. We can try to do the job in one life, and if life is too short, continue in the next. There's always a chance, there has to be an opportunity because life will have no purpose if there isn't. If jail is forever the will to escape is neurotic.

"Ah," I said, "so that's why your meditation is practical. You are trying to scrape bits off your *karma*. Evil *karma* disappears and good *karma* helps you on your way. Your way to where?"

Simon stopped again. "There you go again," he said. "I don't know where I want to go. I want to go *on*, I imagine."

One of the blue jays croaked and Simon pointed at it. "Over there," he said, "look at that blue jay. He is at the beginning of his career. He still has to become a human being. Now I *am* already a human being, but it is no more than another stage. I have to be practical and use my chances so that I can improve my fate. If I don't I may even glide back and become an animal or a bird."

I watched the jays.

Simon shook his head. "No. It can't be true. I don't think we can glide back. Even if we do everything wrong we will still learn. Life must, automatically I suppose, mean an improvement. Every life pushes you a little ahead. What do you think? Do you think you may be a rabbit in your next life?"

"I don't care," I said.

"Would you *want* to be a rabbit, or a squirrel, or a jay?" Simon asked surprised.

"Why not?" I asked.

Simon laughed. His laughter worried me because he wouldn't stop. The tears came into his eyes and he doubled up as if he was in pain.

When he could talk again the words came out slowly. "You are right," he said, "why should I be worried about becoming a rabbit? Why should I think about *karma*? Of course Peter refuses to discuss it."

The grin on his face stayed there till we reached the Zendo. He looked very solemn when he made his bows.

You are eight years old. It is Sunday evening. You have been granted an extra hour before bed.

The family is playing Monopoly. You have been told that you are big enough to join them.

You lose. You are losing continuously. Your stomach cramps with fear. Nearly all your possessions are gone. The money pile in front of you is almost gone. Your brothers are snatching all the houses from your streets. The last street is being sold. You have to give in. You have lost. There is sweat on your forehead.

And suddenly you know that it is only a game. You jump up with joy and you knock the big lamp over. It falls on the floor and drags the teapot with it. The others are angry with you but you laugh when you go upstairs. You know you are nothing, and you know that you have nothing. And you know that not-to-be and not-to-have give an immeasurable freedom.

Later the feeling goes but you remember that you have had it. You know that once, when you were eight years old, you knew freedom.

Sixteen

Moon-faced Buddha II

An old Zen-master in China is approaching his death. A priest comes to visit him and asks the old teacher how he is.

The master answers: "Buddhas with moon-faces, Buddhas with sun-faces."

A text from Peter's holy book, the thin book which once had its own place on the temple-altar in Japan. A book filled with *koans* from the far distant past, a past which can become future again because we live in strange times. In this apparently so well-ordered society, in between the tower-apartments, along the speedways, near the infallibly programmed computers, the masters are returning, and they are as crazy as they used to be, during the times of ancient China, Tibet, India and Japan. A farmer in some cleared land in a forgotten forest, an Armenian selling carpets on the Moscow market, a laborer in a salt mine in North Africa, a street cleaner in Amsterdam, a hermit in the Schwarzwald, the masters are all around us and sometimes we recognize them. The bookshops fill themselves with entire collections of books on "the true meaning of life." Monks in outlandish garb dance and ring their bells in the streets of the capitals. The orthodox monasteries are gradually becoming empty but the communes shoot out of the ground like mushrooms and bamboo stalks.

And somewhere a wise old man dies and mumbles a ridiculous reply to a well-meant question.

"A later master," Peter said, "saw this *koan* and gave his comment. He commented straight from the Absolute and the monk whose mind is in the way does not understand. This is what he said: 'Buddhas with moon-faces, Buddhas with sun-faces.

The five kings.

Bah.

How often didn't they force me to enter the cave of the green dragon?' "

Peter looked at us, the disciples gathered in his livingroom.

"What do you make of this?"

Nobody said anything.

He had half closed his eyes and allowed the silence to enter his room. I knew that he was breathing in a certain way and in deep concentration, that he had bundled his being in the main nerve-knot of his body. Under his black silk robe his belly would be expanded, hard as an iron ball. "Listen with your belly," the old teacher in Kyoto had said. "Think with your belly. Forget your ears, your nose, your eyes. Don't be guided by the imagination of your brain. All answers are right *there*" and he had poked me in the stomach with his short blunt stick. I fell over. The master had laughed. "You aren't sitting well. If you sit properly I could never push you over. You are too wobbly. Go on, go on, bundle your power."

"Buddhas. Emperors. Kings. Bah."

"Nothing matters. The greatest powers of our planet have no real core. We respect kings and emperors and admire the Buddha's example, the man who found freedom. But respect and admiration are limited. Don't be misled. Don't allow yourself to be taken to the 'green dragon's cave' where you can only find your doubts and your fears. The philosophers are in the green dragon's cave, the dragon who is so hard to conquer, and when you have finally fought him to the ground and you are stripping off his hide he has another hide underneath and others underneath that one. The merchants are in the cave, they fight the odds of their existence and sometimes they win but whatever they succeed in grabbing hold of changes into smoke. The generals are in the cave and the politicians. And the Zen disciples. They want to know who is Buddha. They want to have *satori*. We are frightened of the emptiness within and try to fill it. With ideas, with names, with definitions."

And that was the end of Peter's *teisho*. Another extraordinary lecture to be filed away in my memory. Buddhism is said to be negative. We are told what it is not, but never what it is. Don't enter the green dragon's cave. Don't hang yourself on a definition. Don't think that anything at all is important. Don't misuse your power of reasoning.

But meanwhile we are to do the best we can. What task we may find, do it as well as you can. Let the general try to win his battle, the merchant to make his fortune, let the philosopher try to connect his theories and let the engineer invent and use. If the attempt meets with success the result is of no importance. A medal or a rotten tomato, it's all the same. The medal is for your chest, and the tomato may hit you in the face. The resulting smile should be the same.

Rupert was talking to me about the moon-faced Buddhas and the sun-faced Buddhas. We had eaten supper together and washed up and were huddled as close as we could to the smoking stove. We were waiting for the evening meditation, we still had a few minutes.

"It's all very well," Rupert said and stared at me morosely, "but I have been here close to two years and I think I have reached the point where I believe in nothing and doubt everything. And I haven't done badly here. I have even been given a responsible job, leader of the meditation. Boy! What honors. I have had responsible jobs before. I was a psychologist employed by the city council and helped officials whose nerves were giving in. They said I was the right man for the job and my degree was supposed to be a guarantee of success. But I don't know if I ever really helped anybody. I made them do tests and fill in questionnaires and I determined the cause of their symptoms. If I could find out what complex or trauma was bothering them I could prescribe a therapy or change their jobs for them or pat them on the shoulder and wish them luck. It's unbelievable what can go wrong with people and the more intelligent they are the worse the affliction becomes. And success is another factor, success upsets people. Failure is all right, everybody seems to know how to deal with that, it's common, but success is tough luck. And beauty. Beautiful women and handsome men become insane at the drop of a pin."

I looked at my watch, it was almost time. I stretched and yawned. "Come, come, Rupert, my boy," I said, "don't tell sad stories. I am about to sit still for three long hours and I really want to concentrate this time. If you go on like this I'll have a nice vision of an endless row of officials, taking pills to calm their nerves."

Rupert laughed. "That's what I have seen for years. And still, it wasn't such a bad life. You wouldn't say it if you see this cabin but I used to have a lot of books. For years I read, I would devour it all. Literature, religion, psychology, philosophy. You name it, I read it. Before I came here I gave away over thirty cases of books and cartons and cartons of records. My apartment was well furnished. You wouldn't say that either if you see this dump. Perhaps I live in this mess on purpose. I don't read anymore and I don't listen to music and I really like music. Sometimes, when I try to meditate, I hear parts of symphonies, with all the instruments in their places. But I only have three years left here and I am doing exactly as I am told. I meditate and I work and I eat and I sleep and that's it. I work in the sawmill. Stupid work, the same all the time. I must have sawn thousands of trees."

"Three years left?" I asked. "You have to go when they are up?"

"Yes," Rupert said. "When I came here Peter said that he would take me for five years only. Another three years and I get the boot. Maybe he'll allow me to come back, as he is allowing you to come here for a short time but I won't be allowed to live here anymore. This cabin will be for the next disciple."

"And what will you do?" I asked. "Go back to the nervous officials?" We were walking towards the Zendo, he didn't have the car that day.

He didn't answer at first and looked fierce. "It sounds funny," he said, "but when I came here I had the feeling that I had come to the end of the way. I was sure that this, the possibility to work under a Zen master, would be my last chance. And when he said that I would only be able to stay five years I promised myself that, at the end of those five years, I would either have the insight I wanted or commit suicide. I was planning a very spectacular suicide, like blowing myself up, with a hundred pounds of dynamite, right in the center of the Pentagon or some other important center of this sick country."

"An anarchist," I mumbled.

"Yes," Rupert said, "one of these black-bearded guys with sunglasses and plastic bombs in a cardboard suitcase. Anarchism always fascinated me. It's very religious. The Hindus have a special God of Destruction, Shiva the Terrible."

"You still plan to blow yourself up into the sky?" I asked.

"It's all bull," Rupert said, "I knew it then too I guess. But it was an idea I couldn't get rid of at the time. I have lost it now."

"So what do you plan now?"

"Get another apartment," Rupert said, "buy books and records, and furniture and tools for the kitchen."

"What of it?" I asked. "You can't live without all that stuff. I have it too. What's wrong with it anyway?"

"Nothing. I have some possessions even here. Everybody has, the master has a house full of things as well. People give him presents. But he can do without it. A lot of people came here last year, including families, and we couldn't house some of them. Peter gave them his cottage and moved into a small shed himself. He had nothing but a shelf and a little kerosene stove. He lived there for six months and I don't think anybody heard him grumble."

I looked around to see if I could see my friend the squirrel. The conversation began to get on my nerves, I would have preferred silence. It wasn't like Rupert to suddenly break into a stream of words. I noticed that I was looking forward to the meditation. The old teacher in Kyoto had predicted that I would. "One day," he had said, "you will meditate with pleasure. You will do it on your own and nobody will have to force you."

"Will my legs still hurt?" I had asked.

"Of course," the master said, "that pain is forever. It bothers me too. You fold your legs and obstruct the flow of your blood so your feet and legs begin to prickle. And that feeling changes into pain. But it will stop as soon as you walk about for a bit. The pain won't go but it will bother you less and less as your concentration improves. The thoughts are worse than the pain, but they will stop annoying you as well, and you will learn how to deal with sleep. Long sitting in meditation gives deep insight. You don't notice it from day to day because the change is very gradual. But it will come. And then you find that you want to detach yourself from your activity and find a quiet place and sit there by yourself. Now you are forced by time schedules and bells and gongs. After a while you won't need that anymore."

Rupert was still walking next to me looking very despondent. I felt that I should cheer him up.

"Cheer up," I said, "that's it. This will get you nowhere." I patted him on the shoulder.

He scowled at me. "Leave me alone," he said. "People are always petting each other in this place. They even embrace each other nowadays when they meet. Love! Cuddly homosexuals, I don't like that at all!"

"A cuddle in time gives contentment." In Dutch the statement rhymes and while I tried to find a similar rhyme in English, Rupert looked at me as if I had kicked his shin. I tried again.

"Rupert is crazy, Rupert is mad.
The times are dark and the future is bad."

Then I tried to roll over my head in the snow but it didn't come off very well and I got up and rubbed my shoulder. But it had worked, he laughed.

"OK, OK," he said, grinning, "you are doing your best, I can see that. And the future isn't so bad. I still have three years to find out something and after that I can make some money and travel about the world for a while. I could buy a small car or a motorbike and ride around the Far East. I might even locate a holy man who would give me a push."

We were close to the bridge separating the meditation hall from the ordinary world. Once we reached the bridge there could be no more talk.

I waited till we were very close to it. "Do your best Rupert," I said, "you only have three years left." He scowled again and wanted to answer back but I pointed at the bridge we were crossing and put my finger on my lips.

Grinning we reached the Zendo's door.

I did my utmost during the first period trying to reach the strong silence of meditation. Thoughts kept pulling me off and fantasies disturbed the *koan*, a new *koan* I had only just been given. I kept on trying and time went quickly, the pain didn't worry me.

During the five-minute break I kept at it and I entered the second period with the same right intentions. But then I was in Japan. It was such a sudden and extraordinary experience that I had trouble in accepting that I had reached this super-awareness, an awareness of a much higher level than the average trip through space and time we take every day. I really was in Japan but not in the way I had been there ten years earlier. The moments which I now lived, neatly lined up and extremely clear, were the highlights of my memory. I was walking in the narrow shopping street again as I had done once a day, six months long. I smelled the fresh vegetables, the tea, the herbs. I jumped aside for a motorcycle ridden by a young tough with a cotton strip wound around his hair. I walked in the temple gardens, I saw the rocks and the pebbles raked into pleasant patterns but it was more than being aware, there was no distance between the observer and the observed. I met with the old teacher again, I strolled through the red-light quarter of Kobe port, I was in the castle of Osaka, I heard the delicate music of a bamboo flute, I sailed a small boat on Lake Biwa. For a moment I thought that I should break the vision. I hadn't entered the meditation hall to make a trip through Japan, I should solve my *koan*, concentrate on it. But the experience was too stunning. Time had completely disappeared now. Rupert hit his bell and the adventure broke off. I jumped off my cushions and went outside. It was all gone, I could only remember the memory. An unusual abstract experience, consisting of the essence of a year and a half's life. There was no story in the event, no daily routine. An opium dream.

In spite of my right intentions I tried to get back into the adventure during the next period but without any result at all. I gave it up and concentrated. My legs hurt and I trembled. Time passed impossibly slowly, I tried to glance at my watch and the hands had stopped. At last the bell sounded. I didn't go outside but waited standing in front of my seat, miserably. And then I started again.

I understood the *koan*. I didn't know where the answer had come from but it was definitely right. It seemed too simple and I presented it with an effort.

On my way back from *sanzen* I wondered if the master knew what his disciples were going through in the meditation hall. He gave us the *koans*, possibly from the collection printed in the antique *koan* book he kept in his private room. Perhaps, later, he might give me *koans* of his own making. Most masters add to the existing collections. Would he know that I had been in Japan just now? I couldn't tell him. *Sanzen* is formal and restricted to *koans*. There is no conversation at all. There wouldn't be time either, forty disciples take up more than an hour. He was seeing his disciples from five to six hours a day. Two minutes per *sanzen*, that was about all he could give us.

And what are *koans*? Peter had told us, during one of his *teishos* that *koans* are "pointers." I had looked up the word in Simon's fat dictionary. A pointer is a hint, an indication. It's also the stick a teacher will use to indicate something on the blackboard or a map. An aspect of the teaching is pointed at, for a moment. But when you find the *koan*'s answer, as cryptic as the *koan* itself, the interpretation is still yours to find out. The master acknowledges insight, but he doesn't tell you what to do with your insight. The *koans* indicate a direction but you can still improvise. You may even go along a way which the master doesn't approve of, and he may terminate your training. But your insight will still be right and properly acknowledged.

How do you handle insight? *Koans* aren't games with words, there is no cleverness, no ingenuity in the interchange between master and disciple. The answer comes straight from meditation, it pops up, like a live rabbit from a magician's hat. What will you do with the live rabbit? Train it? Eat it? Some of the rabbits I produced I didn't like at all.

I came home mumbling to myself. Rupert had made his favorite health drink, hot aniseed milk with a blob of honey, sprinkled over with nutmeg, a revolting looking mixture which tastes good. I drank the hot sweet thick liquid, resting my head against the wall.

"So how is my friend this evening?" Rupert asked.

I shook my head and took another sip.

"It isn't easy, what?"

"No," I said, "what on earth are we trying to do?"

"Beats me," Rupert said, "but we may as well go on. Have some more."

I held up my mug.

But although the reason of our activity eluded us, it did make us very tired and I was asleep before i had put my head on the blankets.

Three thousand million people live on a ball.

The ball is suspended in nothing.

What are these three thousand million people doing on the ball?

And why, Mr. Zen Student, do you want to know?

You don't know that either.

Seventeen

The marabou

"Good afternoon."

"I woke up, trying, vainly, to grab hold of a shred of dream rapidly drifting off.

"Excuse my intrusion."

I didn't know who was talking to me and I couldn't see anything.

It was during the afternoon break and I had sneaked into the dark hole under my blankets after a lonely lunch, consisting of a bit of turkey spine and some bread baked in the settlement. Rupert hadn't come home.

"Can I help you?" the same voice said and I now saw its owner. My colleague-writer, the man I had met in the bungalow belonging to Peter's friends, the day after Rohatsu.

"Please excuse me," my visitor said, "you had a blanket over your head and I pulled it off."

I must have given him a black look for he began to apologize again.

"Please excuse this intrusion. I wanted to see you but it is very difficult to make contact with anyone here. There is no telephone either. I knocked on a few doors and finally traced you to this cabin. I only want to make an appointment so that I can come back later, at a convenient time."

I had slept deeply and it took a few moments before I could form a sentence. I got up and shook my head, I had to shake it a few times before my brain cleared.

"I was asleep," I said, "but you are welcome. I always try to get some sleep in the afternoon, if I have a chance that is."

"Yes," the man said, "you get up very early, I know that. But allow me to introduce myself. My name is James."

He extended a cool dry hand. I paid a little more attention now. A neat man, dressed in a blue striped suit, complete with waistcoat. A gray tie. Watery blue eyes behind thick glasses. A good figure, very good for his age, he must have been over sixty years old. I shook my head again.

"Would you like some tea?"

"No, no," James said, "don't trouble yourself. I only want to make an appointment, you go back to sleep. I'll be back when you have some time and feel like talking to me."

I glanced at Rupert's alarm, we had an hour before the meditation would start again. I was awake now anyway.

"You can stay if you like. We have an hour. I am going to make tea, have some."

He was wearing a wig, or part of a wig. The hair at the sides and the back of his head seemed real but the piece covering his cranium could be false. It was too well arranged.

The tea was ready in a few minutes, I had put a kettle on the stove before going to sleep.

"You are a writer aren't you?" I asked.

"So are you?" James asked.

"Not really," I said.

He puckered his lips. "You are a writer or you aren't. You have a book in the bookstores, haven't you?"

"Yes," I said.

"Then you are a writer."

"I chopped some wood this morning," I said, and poured the tea, "but I don't think I am a wood chopper."

James stirred his tea with a bent spoon. There was no chair in the house. He was still standing in the place where I had first seen him when I woke up. I folded some blankets and put them on the floor.

"Please sit down."

"Thank you."

I looked at him with amazement. He had sat down in one movement, it looked as if he had dropped his body on the floor, but he was sitting well, legs crossed, and he hadn't spilled a drop of his tea.

"Your body is very supple."

James smiled. I saw two lines of slightly irregular, very white teeth and estimated them to have cost a few thousand dollars. He pulled up his trousers with his free hand.

"I exercise daily, keeps me fit."

I sat down as well and stirred my tea. We observed each other in silence.

"But if you aren't a writer, then what are you?" The watery eyes held me kindly but firmly.

I had to think of a remark Peter had made that morning. We had worked together for an hour, pulling cut trees on to a clearing behind his house. We were close to a path and every time someone came past he had stopped working and asked, in a loud voice, "How are you this morning?" Almost everyone had answered with "Fine, and how are you?" except Edgar who had mumbled something, taken off his fur cap, pulled it inside out and put it on again. He had made me laugh for the lining of his cap was made of a red material dotted with white blobs and this new headgear had looked very funny on Edgar's round red head.

"Is that the right answer?" I had asked Peter.

"Not bad."

"I didn't ask that," I had said. "Is it the right answer?"

"Not yet."

He hadn't answered my further questions.

One can behave in a normal fashion, and one can behave in a crazy fashion. The Zen masters and the Zen disciples whom we meet in literature always choose the crazy way. They ask each other mad questions, they beat each other up, and they laugh a lot.

But only the book people behave that way. In real life the Zen men behave like most sane men. I had been able to observe them for some length of time in Japan and they seemed to function along accepted patterns. They made appointments, did as they were told by those higher in rank, worked in the kitchen or the gardens, and

meditated during set hours. I hadn't noticed any stunning irregu-
larities. The crazy part of their lives was limited to the *koans* and
the ever recurring interview with the master. But there had been
some exceptions—a sudden remark, an unfinished sentence, and
some experiences which could not be explained straight off.

I thought that I could understand Peter's game with the disciples.
He asked them how they were. It would interest him how they
were, of course. But to ask, "How are you this morning" is a stan-
dard question, a form without much meaning, or depth.

But the question can be quite deep.

"How are you? How are you, tramp of the universe? How are
you, apparent identity? How are you, Bodhisattva, you, who have
sworn to reach Nirvana? How are you, asker of many questions?
Are you awake today? Do you know why you are walking along
that track in the forest? Do you know what you are doing?"

Only Edgar had understood that Peter had asked more than he had
seemed to ask. But Edgar hadn't known how to express a proper
answer. That's why he had mumbled something and had performed
the little act with his cap. Not bad. But not quite right either.

But what should he have done? Should he have rushed at Peter
and slapped the master's face?

Should he have shouted "*om*" or some other powerful mantra?

And what was I supposed to do now? A very neat gentleman, the
writer James, the intruder who had disturbed my afternoon's sleep,
this being who used a costly and nimble body, wanted to know
what I was, and perhaps he even wanted to know who I was. Why
would he want to know?

Was he a practicing author, looking for material for his next
novel? Or did he want to know what we were doing here to make
some mystical profit out of the meeting?

When I had met him before he had seemed to be very intelligent.
He had been the only one to grasp that Peter was kidding the
hostess. The beings living on Mount Meru were equipped with
wings which would begin to rot after a while. Even the blessed lives
come to an end. Reincarnation offers no comfort. You may go to

heaven for a bit but what happens when your stretch is up? Will you have to face another painful birth? Will it start all over again? And who will guarantee that you will never have to go to hell? And suppose you are lucky and are drafted from one heaven to another, won't you be disturbed by the thought that billions of beings will suffer somewhere else?

The writer, who now turned out to be called James, had understood the point of the story.

"All right," I said, for James was still looking at me. "I am a writer. You are a writer as well. But you haven't come to ask me whether I am a writer or not. Why did you come?"

Perhaps I should have asked him to play a round of poker with me. He would be very good at it. The expression of his face didn't change. He produced a gold cigar case. I took a cigar.

A gold cigar case. They are rare nowadays. I expected the car which would be waiting for him on Rupert's driveway to be an imported French car of the most expensive type.

"When I met you before you were also smoking a cigar," James said, "and you were drinking a martini, I believe."

Don't be caught, I told myself. Act innocently. Don't be tricked into the defensive.

"Yes," I said pleasantly, "a cigar and a martini."

The conversation halted again. What would he be thinking? Would he believe that the faithful belonging to this particular creed discipline themselves and abstain from the joys which our society offers so freely?

Let him say it himself, I thought.

James sucked his cigar and blew a ring, a nicely shaped ring.

"You really must excuse me," he said, "I know I have no right whatever to barge into your privacy. But I am curious, as you will understand. Writers are always curious. The meeting with your master, Peter, and with yourself, has impressed me. I would like to know a little more. I am sure that I haven't come to Earth by accident. I believe that because I am a positive person, like most Americans. We are simple souls, perhaps that's the reason that our country is so powerful. Our forefathers came to this continent because they were looking for profit. They could gain nothing in their native countries and meant to find their fortune here. We, Americans, made our fortune. The fact cannot be disputed. For years the United States has been the richest country of the world. It still is. But to be rich isn't everything."

"No," I said.

"Are you rich?" my guest asked.

"Sure."

James laughed. "You say that very nicely. If you ask anyone here if he is rich he will avoid the question. Even if he lives in a palatial home and spends most of his weekends in Miami, even if he can influence the stock market he will refuse to say that he is rich."

"Perhaps they think that they can become even richer," I said.

"Of course," James said. "That's why. You can always add a little to your pile. But you can lose your pile too and that can be very worrying. And perhaps these people are superstitious, they don't want to tempt fate. So you are rich?"

"Sure," I said.

"How do you mean?" James said. "How would you define rich?"

"Oh," I said, and made a vague gesture.

James shook his head carefully. "No. You mustn't avoid the question. I promise to give honest answers to everything you may ask me. Perhaps this conversation may be of use to you. You know that nothing happens without reason. I came here and you received me politely, you gave me a seat, tea and the use of your time. You know that I came here with a purpose. And now I ask you a few questions. What do you mean by rich?"

Bah, I thought. I should be having my nap and here I am, awake, and in conversation with a neat gentleman, and intelligent to boot.

"Are you ready?" Peter had asked and I had answered, "For what?" and he had shaken his head. A good question and a silly answer. You always have to be ready. I would have to be ready *now* to conduct this conversation.

"Rich," I said hesitatingly. "I say I am rich. And I am, without any doubt. I have clothes, food, a roof over my head. I even own a car and some savings. And an income. But that isn't what you mean."

He shook his head.

"So you know the answer to your own question. I have what you have."

His watery eyes showed some life. "And what do I have?"

But now I had him cornered. "You said you would answer honestly. If you don't know what I mean you should say so, but I think you know what I mean."

"All right," James said, "you win. I have the same chance as you have. The human chance. We can become free. That's tremendous wealth. It is the right, and at the same time the possibility, of every human being. I take it that that's what you mean?"

I must have nodded for he went on.

"But these are words. We are now discussing liberty. Now what's liberty?"

No, no, I thought. These questions are beyond me. It should be a *sanzen* question. I might meditate on it and perhaps I would find some sort of answer, satisfactory perhaps, for a while. And then the problem would be touched in a new *koan*. But this wasn't *sanzen*. James wanted me to answer him now and he wanted a reasonable answer.

"Nirvana," I said, without much hope.

"It's another word," James said.

"Now tell me what Nirvana is."

I had asked the old teacher in Japan and he had pointed at the floor. "Here," he had said, "you are there already. You are in Nirvana. You are like a fish claiming it is thirsty. You are right in the middle of it. Here. Here."

But I couldn't tell James that he was in Nirvana already. I might as well be honest.

"Listen," I said and James immediately changed his expression to one of extreme attention. He was listening. I had to laugh and he laughed as well.

"Listen," I said again and he stopped laughing and became attentive again. "Now listen here. I don't know what Nirvana is. I don't even know if it really exists. If I have digested what I have read and heard, Nirvana should be the sphere where we are free. Who has reached Nirvana never has to be born again, not on Earth, not on another planet, not in the hereafter, not in heaven and not in hell. Whoever has reached Nirvana, *is there*. Do you follow?"

"No," James said.

"I don't either," I said, "and that's why I am here."

James held up a hand. "Just a minute," he said. "I want to interrupt you a minute. You aren't new to this training I believe. Have you been in it for a long time?"

But what is a long time? A year? Ten years? Old people say that life doesn't take long. "I don't know what a long time is," I said.

He looked at me.

"No, no," I said hurriedly. "I am not avoiding the question. I really don't know what a long time is. I am not new to this training. But time doesn't mean much. There may be disciples here who have made real progress, who are advanced, experts if you like."

"You are being modest," James said.

"Sure. It's always clever to be modest."

"Cleverness is nonsense," James said.

"It's all nonsense."

James looked out of the window. "It's all nonsense," he repeated, "very true. A true Buddhist saying. The Taoists claimed the same. And even the Christians. When Eckhart was asked about God he wouldn't answer. He said something about there being no God, but no no-God either. He must have made the remark out of that Nirvana of yours."

"Nirvana isn't mine," I said.

James sighed. "You must excuse an old man for asking all these questions."

"You aren't old."

He smiled and bowed slightly. "Very kind of you. I keep fit but I am an old man. I have a small but very complete collection of medicines in my car. My body is gradually falling to bits. The combination of the various diseases I am suffering from will kill me within the next five or ten years. I have read and thought a lot and now, rather suddenly, I have run into this movement and met a master and I am impressed. I am not easily impressed. I have always preferred to be cynical and I have nearly always been proved right in the end, although there were a few exceptions. I met an old gardener once, and my best friend had a remarkable grandmother. I have, indeed, met some impressive people but very few of them. The 'masters' I have met or sought out, the clairvoyants and holy men and truth-spouters . . . they were quacks, no other word would suit them. They want you to join their club and admire them and you should pay them of course. I don't think your master would accept my money."

"No," I said.

"Does he accept yours?"

"Yes," I said, "but that's an honor."

"He asks for money?"

"A small monthly contribution. And only disciples are allowed to pay. If the disciple doesn't please him he returns the money."

"Has it ever happened?"

"Yes," I said.

"That's good," James said, "very good. A real man."

"What's a real man?"

James got up. My question seemed to have touched him. He lost his self-discipline for a moment. For a few seconds he wasn't the beautiful expensive elderly gentleman but seemed lost, nervous. He made a half-finished gesture.

"A real man is the man the Bible describes. The last man who is the first. He will give you his last cigarette. He will visit you when you are ill, or when the world has proved you to be a fool and you are alone, in a corner. The man who helps without wanting to be a helper. A man who can't grab because he's got nothing to grab with."

"Hmm," I said, "you are describing the village idiot."

"Quite," James said, "you could be very right. Never underestimate the village idiot. Or the retarded and the silly."

I thought of the storekeeper in the nearby town and his retarded son. "Peter is friendly with a retarded young man."

"You see," James said. "Could I have some more tea? It's very dry in this cabin."

I filled his mug and he looked at me contentedly. "Don't you have to go yet?"

I looked at the alarm. It was about time. "Have you ever meditated?" I asked.

"No," James said, "but I have been doing Yoga exercises for several years. I can sit in the full lotus."

"Why don't you join us this afternoon? I can ask the meditation leader for permission. We only sit for two hours now, and there are several breaks."

James got up.

"You coming?" I asked.

He nodded.

I hadn't thought he would. It's easy to find someone who wants to discuss Buddhism but meditation is something else. The idea of having to sit still is frightening, the victim feels caught and worries about visions and nervous tension.

We were just in time and Rupert was in his seat at the end of the hall. I asked James to wait at the entrance and walked to the altar, turned on my heels, faced Rupert and bowed. He bowed back. That I knew Rupert well didn't count here. Here he was the jikki, the absolute leader, the temple's boss.

"I have a guest who wants to join in the afternoon's meditation. Will that be all right?"

We were whispering, behind me I could feel the eyes of the fierce Bodhisattva statue, holding his sword which cuts all thought.

"Can he sit still?" Rupert asked.

"He says he can."

"O.K."

I walked back to the entrance where James was quietly waiting, holding himself stiffly, hands behind his back.

"It's all right. You can come in. Bow at the entrance and fold your hands. Do everything I do, I'll show you your seat."

He nodded.

Rupert pointed at the seat next to me, apparently Edgar had been excused for the afternoon.

James sat very quietly, four times twenty-five minutes. I heard his peaceful breathing.

We walked back together.

"That was very pleasant," James said, "very restful. I feel a lot better."

"What were you doing while you sat there?"

"Yes," James said. "What was I doing? I dreamt a little about my youth. I tried to breathe as slowly as possible. I thought about our conversation and during the last period I concentrated."

"On what?"

James grinned.

I could imagine what he must have looked like as a young man. The striped suit, the expensive gold watch, the wig, the disciplined good manners became transparent.

"I concentrated on the unimportant. All my life I have been interested in the eastern religions and methods although I have always remained a Christian. The emptiness of Buddhism and Taoism fascinates me. To be empty, to know that nothing matters. Do you know that? Do you know that nothing matters?"

I looked serious and said that I knew, but then I qualified my statement. I said that I *suspected* it.

"Yes, yes," James said as if he hadn't heard me. "It's the truth. Nothing matters. That Buddha of yours doesn't matter either. Neither does my Christ, or Mohammed or Ramakrishna. None of the prophets, the sons of God. Nirvana itself doesn't matter. And we matter least of all. Self is the absolute joke. It goes even further. Emptiness, the mysterious Tao, the Stone the alchemists looked for, the teaching of the witches. . . ."

He interrupted himself. "Witches can really do tricks, do you know? They can fly and change themselves into objects and animals. This is indeed a strange life, full of possibilities."

"I don't know anything about witches," I said, "but I am quite prepared to believe that they can fly."

"Yes," James said, "but it is of no real importance. There is, I have thought that for a long time, longer than I can remember, maybe from the first moment I could think, nothing more fascinating than the idea that only the really indifferent can win."

I moved aside a little so that there was more distance between us. I studied the way he walked. Marabous walk like that, I thought. The birds of prey, tall and stately, which I had seen in the zoo and on film.

Not a bad comparison, I thought. He is the bird of prey, and I am the prey. He rips the flesh of my bones. I don't matter, and my idea of Buddhism doesn't matter either. Nirvana itself is of no importance. Whatever I do is empty, and even emptiness is neither the beginning, nor the end, nor the goal of our existence. Whatever I try to hold on to has no substance.

"You have to let go," James was saying now, "that's what reading about Buddhism has taught me. Whenever you try to hold on to something you are lost. You will be ripped to pieces and it hurts. But to let go is not easy. Perhaps it's the most difficult action for us who have to live in this world. To learn how to let go must be the supreme effort. I don't envy you your training."

I saw his car now, he hadn't parked it on Rupert's driveway but further along, in between some trees. It was indeed an exceptional car, an old Bentley, a status symbol *par excellence*.

"Ah," James said, "there's my car. It's time to thank you for your hospitality. You have been of great help to me. Here is my card. I am driving back to New York now. Perhaps you will look me up one day."

"Thank you," I said. "and what are you going to do now?"

"Continue living," James said, "or would you want me to give it all up and live here, in this commune?"

"I don't want anything," I said.

"You are trying not to want anything," James corrected. "But that's very commendable. You must do the very best you can. And then you will come to the place where you can let everything go."

"And then I have arrived," I said morosely.

"Exactly," James said.

I wished him a good journey. He allowed me to hold his dry cool hand again. The engine ignited and the Bentley drove off.

"You have expensive friends," a voice said behind me.

It was Edgar. His cap was still inside out.

"Your cap is inside out."

"Yes," Edgar said, "that won't be necessary now." He took his cap off and changed it into a fur cap. "Who is your expensive friend?"

"He is called James and he writes books," I said and walked away quickly.

"Hey!" Edgar shouted but I didn't stop. I had had enough for one day.

You meet someone.

The other.

You meet the other.

You are polite. The other is polite.

You eat each other a little.

After his departure you are slightly damaged.

And what do you do then?

Do you repair the damage and do you become again what you were?

Or do you go on as you are?

Damaged, but lighter.

Eighteen

The geese

It was 7:00 a.m. and I stood on the veranda of Rupert's cabin. I had just come back from the morning's meditation and didn't feel like going inside where the cold dank room was waiting for me. I would have to wash up and prepare breakfast, and sweep the floor and set the table, and, worst of all, persuade the stove to burn instead of smoke.

I had a few minutes. Rupert would be due in half an hour's time, he had gone to do some repairs on the antique truck's engine powering the sawmill. There was no need to go in straightaway, I could smoke and think a little.

But it was cold and I felt the need of a little movement. I stamped my feet and the boards of the veranda responded with a deep hollow sound. I tried again and the sound got even better. The stamping grew into a slow dance and I began to hum and clap my hands. I laughed, and stopped. A dancing dervish. Dancing can be very religious. The dervishes lost their ego while they twirled and howled. Buddhist monks are also known to dance. The Tibetans have their lama dances and the Zen priests go in for intricate ceremonial jigs, I had seen them do these in the court of the magnificent main temple of our sect in Kyoto. But dancing isn't the main occupation of Zen monks. They prefer to meditate. Long meditation gives deep insight. One of Peter's statements, one of his very few, coming from his own experience.

I tried to calculate how many hours I had meditated. Three thousand perhaps. Or four? Is that a lot?

And did I have this deep insight now?

Sure, sure, I told myself. Don't be too modest. You do have

insight, dear boy. It won't be very much and there will be others who have more insight, a couple of billion times more, but that subtle point can be ignored. Insight is insight. You know why you are alive. No, I said, I don't know why I am alive. I have merely stopped asking myself, because I have stopped caring. The question has disappeared. But questions only disappear because they have been answered. So what was the answer?

Not to be expressed in words. I said cleverly. Real wisdom can never be expressed in words. Don't be clever, I told myself.

All right, I said. I have understood, or I have begun to understand that "I" do not exist. Which means that "my life" does not exist either. And you don't have to ask about the purpose of something which isn't there.

You are still being clever, I said. And I was right. But how should I handle this? How can the inexpressible be expressed? How are moments of insight described? How do you indicate that you are on the right path?

Buddhism is negative. It will tell you what it is not. When you insist that it must be something it merely allows for an open space, which you can fill in as you like. It is only specific about its method. It tells you to meditate, to be conscious of what you are doing, to do your best. It tells you to earn your daily food in a decent manner. It prescribes kind speech and thought. It suggests that you should create your own situations, rather than being pushed around by yourself and others. It warns that you should not avoid your own doubts. It recommends trying things out for yourself. It abhors all dogma. It doesn't like you to impose your opinions on others. And it stresses that you should know yourself, your own laziness, pride and greed which, together, constitute the power which turns the wheel of life.

One moment, I told myself. I do know something. I know that freedom exists. It seems to be the central point of Buddhism. The turning wheel seems eternal. Life follows life, heaven follows heaven, hell follows hell. The will to live creates new births and new deaths. But freedom can be reached at any given moment. The Buddha liberated himself, the Zen masters liberated themselves. Whatever they could do you can as well. You have to keep on trying.

Are you sure? I asked. Did you experience this freedom? And if you did, what is it? Is freedom symbolized by sitting on a cloud, as the Buddha did on the posters which you saw in Ceylon? You sit on a cloud, free from all influence of the wheel of life, and you watch the endeavor of the little people who are still rummaging about in the limited space of their egos? And where is that cloud anyway?

Well, the cloud is here. The cloud isn't outside your life. You shouldn't look too far. Freedom is right here, where it has always been. When you try to escape you make a silly mistake. But how do you know that this freedom exists?

Freedom exists, I said stubbornly.

Are you frightened now? I asked. Did I touch the sore spot in your faith? Do you want to stop this discussion? Are you losing your temper because I am kicking against the shelf which supports your importance? Do you think the shelf may break and that you will drop into the bottomless hole? Are you worried about losing something?

No. I wasn't frightened. Freedom exists and will go on forever. Freedom is not connected with the ego. Whether the ego believes in it or not, it will always be there. It's outside illusion.

"What's for breakfast?" Rupert asked.

I looked up.

"Have you lost your mind?" Rupert asked. "I came walking up the track and waved at you and you looked straight through me. I shouted, 'GOOD MORNING!' and you were watching me with empty eyes."

"What's for breakfast?"

"Empty eyes?" I asked.

"Forget it," Rupert said, "you had empty eyes. Only the whites showed, not the pupils."

"No pupils?"

"Bah," Rupert said, "don't irritate me. I made a joke. I want to know what's for breakfast. I am hungry. Peter wants me to do something for him in town. I have ten minutes for breakfast. 'WHAT DO YOU HAVE TO EAT?'

"Nothing," I said pleasantly.

He stamped on the floor. He was angry, no doubt about it. He had nearly lost his temper a few times during the month I had lived in his cabin but he had always managed to grab hold of it in time, but now he definitely lost it. "What the hell were you doing all this time? You had half an hour at least didn't you?"

"I was thinking."

"About what?"

"About freedom."

"And you made no breakfast? Do you want me to eat your freedom?"

I had kept the pleasant expression on my face and Rupert narrowed his eyes. "OK So I won't eat. I have to go."

"Can I give you some money? You can have breakfast on the way."

Rupert narrowed his eyes a little more. His hands became fists and he came close. "I don't need your money. You are a spoiled turd. You don't belong here. You can't live on five dollars a week. Your life is too easy. You hop in a plane and you slip into your fur coat and you play your game. You'll never get anywhere like this. You'll get ideas."

He walked to the car which he had parked at the beginning of the track. The car was beyond the curve and I heard him slam its door; the engine roared, the tires squealed, and I heard a loud bump. When I walked down the track to find out what had happened the car had already disappeared but its tracks collided with a tree. The tree had lost some of its bark. Rupert's car would have a good-sized dent. It would cost some fifty dollars to repair it, and the door might be damaged as well.

I walked back to the cabin and prepared breakfast. I made a feast of it, eating his share of the sausages as well. Anger is a disease, I thought as I helped myself to another egg. A disease as common as the cold. I suffered from it myself. You shout and stamp and you are convinced you are right and your car hits a tree. You press a button and bombs drop out of an airplane. You throw napalm at running soldiers and set fire to hospitals and schools. You telephone the police and charge your neighbor with a crime. You climb on a soapbox and wave your hands. You have a nasty taste in your mouth and after a while your stomach develops ulcers.

I wasn't angry with Rupert. He was right, of course. I should have prepared breakfast on time. I would try to do better tomorrow. Now it was too late. I buttered some more toast.

"Where is Rupert?"

Peter had come in and was trying to warm his hands at our un-helpful stove.

"He drove off in a huff. I had forgotten to make breakfast and he didn't have time to wait."

Peter laughed and sat down on the floor at the other side of the makeshift table. I poured him some tea.

"Did he shout at you?"

"Yes," I said with my mouth full, "he called me a spoiled turd, life is too easy for me, I can't learn anything."

Peter nodded.

"Is he right?"

"No," Peter said. "You can learn all right. But he is correct when he claims that your life is easy. You'll be gone in a few days' time. Rupert can't go away. He has the idea that he has to stay here for years. Life can be pleasant out here but it can be very tiring, de-pressing even. He has to get up at 2:30 almost every morning. I make him do heavy manual labor. And he meditates."

I began to clear the table and poured some water in the sink for the washing-up. "Ordinary life isn't so easy either."

Peter picked up a dishtowel. He patted me on the shoulder. "Poor fellow. All that responsibility you have to put up with. I sympathize with you."

"I sympathize with you too," I said.

When we had done the washing up I began to sweep the floor but Peter stopped me.

"You can leave that," he said. "I need you this morning. You can help me take the geese to their new house. The others are all working in the forest and I can't handle the geese by myself."

I suddenly thought of Edgar telling me that Peter had been

bumped on the head the year before by a tree which he had chopped down himself.

"I say, Peter. I heard that you had an accident last year. A tree fell on you and knocked you out. Is that true?"

Peter looked at me. "Who told you?"

"I can't remember now," I said.

"It's true," Peter said. "I am always telling everyone never to chop down trees by themselves. When the tree hits you and you are alone you may lie around in the snow for a few hours until you are found. Or you may not be found at all and freeze to death. It nearly happened to me."

"That wasn't very intelligent," ı said.

"No."

"So Zen masters make mistakes?" I asked.

"Ah. That's what you are driving at?"

I didn't say anything.

"Well, you are right. Zen masters make mistakes."

I shook my head.

"Does that put you off?"

"Yes," I said. "I don't mind if I make mistakes but there should be someone around who doesn't."

"Why?" Peter asked.

"Makes me feel better."

He laughed. "Well, I am afraid the masters won't help you that way. They teach, and meanwhile they are bumped on the head by their own trees."

"Never mind," he said a little later, when we were walking on the highway, "this will cheer you up again. Chasing geese is very amusing work, you'll see."

Geese are loud-beaked stupid birds. Peter owned a flock of twenty. We had to drive them across the highway and about a mile of fields. They lost their direction, gaggled and honked. A few tried to fly but they were too heavy and dropped back into the snow. Geese also have the Buddha nature but I had some difficulty in noticing it. I shouted, rushed up and down and hit them on their fat bottoms with a twig.

"What are you going to do with these geese?"

"Fatten them," Peter said, "and then into the pot."

"Are you going to kill them yourself?"

"No," Peter said, "I couldn't. Somebody from the town will have to do it."

A real Buddhist, I thought. The Tibetans had to import Muslims to kill their cattle as no Tibetan wanted to be a butcher. A butcher accumulates a lot of bad *karma* and it may hinder him on the path. But there's nothing wrong in eating meat off a body which has been clobbered to death by another.

I had to laugh on the way. The geese managed a mass breakthrough and wobbled back as fast as they could. Peter cut them off and herded them my way again and they approached me, neatly arranged with Peter behind them, his arms stretched out, hollering at the top of his voice. His cap rested on the back of his head and his mouth was wide open. His face was gleaming with sweat.

"Good show, what?" he asked as he came past me.

Life is a good show.

Amusing, full of jokes.

Life is a joke the old Japanese teacher in Kyoto had said. He had been very serious about it.

Men are born, suffer, and die.

They are hungry, they linger in concentration camps, they are afflicted with leprosy and cancer, they live in small concrete rooms in homes for the aged, they cry with fear when their house are bombed. They drown like rats. They buy things they don't need which break after a short while. Whatever you can imagine will happen, sooner or later. Man is spared nothing. He suffers in the most intricate ways. He can even go mad and will be given pills and he is dazed for a while but when the pills stop working man is mad again. But life is a joke. I knew it. I knew something. But not enough. Curiosity, or doubt, forced me to go on. That afternoon I would meditate again. And that evening. A sovereign remedy, prescribed by the Zen masters.

Nineteen

A corpse

It was time to go back. You have other things to do than sit still in a blockhouse in the snow.

In Amsterdam your bourgeois existence waits patiently. It knows you'll be back. Your family, your home, your job, the daily trip to the office and the warehouse, the waiting for traffic lights, the quick glance at the clock in the churchtower. You are a little late today, you are nicely on schedule today.

The shopping list awaits you and the ringing telephones and the morning's mail. The routine, the rut.

The monotony of daily life had once been the curse of your existence, the most gruesome vision your imagination could shape for you. The thought that your life would be filled with a series of endlessly repeated motions seemed unbearable. You wanted anything except that. You had wanted to find a tension which would have to be increased continuously until, one day, you would burst. The possibility that you might break your mind, or have an accident, seemed a release. You had cheered yourself with the idea that life is a trip leading onto a precipice. The precipice would be an adventure in itself, and you would enjoy the final fall.

You were convinced that you really believed that. The jump into Buddhism had seemed connected with your imaginations. You had some vague ideas when you jumped. Monastic life was a heroic meeting with the High, or the Deep.

Adventure and heroism. The words are associated with "sensational experience." That's what you had been after. Perhaps you were hunting for visions, perhaps you wanted to see the Bodhisattvas in their many aspects, lovely and evil, seducing and torturing.

A corpse

Perhaps you had thought that the monks would make music and that the master near his altar would increase the vibrations within the temple until insight would be torn from your soul. Perhaps you had meant to float towards heaven, or Nirvana, in an incense cloud while the priests banged away on their gigantic temple drums.

And something had happened. The monks had made weird music. The priests had banged away on their drums, drums like wine casks, with tightened skins held into place by large copper nails. The drummer scraped his sticks over the nails and your hair stood on end. And the master prostrated himself on the floor, again and again, humbling himself while the life-sized Buddhas on the altar watched him, active in their eternal smiling peace, while the coiling incense smoke joined the master's frail body to the compassionate divinities.

You had visions as well.

And perhaps some insight had been produced, a little insight which may have been deepened in this landscape of snow and bare trees.

"So what did you learn?" I ask.
"Nothing," you say.
You say: "Dear friend, I have learned nothing."
But such a modest answer is a great arrogance. Only Nothing *is*, and if anyone pretends to know this Nothing he must be mistrusted at sight because he uses big words and pretends to be on such a high level that I can only shake my head and continue my way through the void which still seems full.

You see that your answer hasn't reached me and you try again.
Now you say that you have felt this Nothing.

But the statement is still too lofty, too arrogant. Nothing is the great mystery. It cannot be described. Words can try to touch it. Zen may be such a word and Tao, Christ, Allah, Buddha, are others. There is a word called "God."

176

A corpse

These words can be written down. I can form sentences with them. I can think of theories and fit the words in. But the words are of another order than the imaginable order I am in.

A Zen master says that Buddha is a piece of dogshit. Meister Eckhart denies the existence of God and no-God. Christ appears in a Dutch novel disguised as a waiter with rabbit's teeth. All these descriptions are right, and wrong.

I ask you what you have learned.

You did learn something, didn't you? You aren't in this because you have nothing else to do? The monk who spends ten hours a day sitting still in an uncomfortable cold hall, why does he do that?

You are looking at me. You aren't saying anything. You mean I have to think it out for myself? You mean that there are truths the size of cows and that these truths have been staring me in the face since the moment I was born?

You mean that I should know that I should do my best? Because I am a Dutchman? To do your utmost, it's a truth the size of a Dutch cow.

We are a diligent people. Plain stupid diligence is out of fashion now but many an example can still be found in this sloppy draughty swamp.

You mean I should stay at it, doing my utmost, until death grabs me by the neck?

Allow me to laugh a little, won't you? It was the last thing you expected when Buddhism confirmed to you that you should do your best. You resisted the message until it was very clear indeed. The being called "human" must do his best. Whatever he does, he must do it well. And he should be indifferent.

But that sounds difficult to me. I am born in the West. I want a plain truth. How can I be indifferent while doing my best?

I might understand if I was born in the East. Wisdom comes a little more naturally in the East. A Chinese spends a lifetime on his vegetable gardens but the floods come and sweep them away and the Chinese stands on a hilltop and smiles and waits for the floods to go, and starts all over again.

Could I manage that smile if I reach the Buddha's mountain and there is nothing there?

Anything else you know now?

Yes, perhaps. A Tibetan monk told you about "loving-kindness," the Buddha's compassion and his endless understanding. You got into the story easily enough. Kindness can be understood. But you couldn't connect the kindness with the training of Zen. The training seemed tough, just tough. You had to sit still and concentrate and you couldn't even complain. But later you thought that you might understand. Zen masters are very kind.

If something doesn't work they stop. Monks and disciples are told to leave. Meditation periods are lengthened, without explanation. You have been given something to do and you are interested and you are told to do something else. You are praised and put in charge of others and then, suddenly, it's all over again and the master doesn't seem to know you when you meet him in the garden.

But his acts are acts of kindness. He works from a point which you can't reach or grasp. He is free, and you are not. He knows what is going on. You doubt his wisdom at times. Disciples are leaving him, and they come back, or not. Anything goes, anything has a purpose.

There is no purpose at all, a truth the size of a cow. You do your utmost. What you have imagined takes shape. You become rich, you are successful, people admire you. But circumstances change and you are no longer admired. It is proved, beyond the slightest doubt, that you were wrong from the beginning. The general is retired well before his time. The tycoon leaves for Switzerland or he hangs himself leaving a short and bitter note. The writer is forgotten and the actor waits for his applause. The ballet dancer dies in a lunatic asylum and the statesman is jailed.

And whatever you do, you will die. Anything you manage to build will be broken down again, sometimes while you are still around. The day will come that your life's work is unravelled, right to the last bit of thread.

Even the ball you live on offers no security. Planets disappear and every day some new planets are formed. We live in a void, a void without purpose.

So it's all a joke. The old teacher was very serious about it. He told you that you would understand what he meant one day, and you believed him.

So maybe now you are beginning to understand. But you don't dare to be sure yet. Maybe something will happen today, or tomorrow, which will shake your "insight." But you don't worry about it as much as you did. You'll see what will happen and meanwhile you continue.

Now you can understand that there was a Zen master once who sat down at the side of the road and roared with laughter every time someone happened to pass him. Some declared him crazy and walked off but others stopped to ask him what was so amusing. He didn't explain, he just laughed. He didn't laugh at them, he laughed because of what he saw. And he lived in a time of oppression, of misery, of famine. In India yogis meditate for years on end. They don't eat, they don't sleep and they don't go to the toilet. They sit under a tree, or in a cave or on a rubbish dump near a big city. They live in silence and their silence radiates charity; perhaps the roaring laughter of the Zen master was charitable as well.

Life is misery, and miraculous beauty. The word "miracle" has been used too often and has lost its value. But we live in miracles. The thrushes in the park, the ducks drifting on the canals, the floating seagulls, but also the car on the highway, the mechanical digger in the polder and the large square apartment blocks. Whoever can take the time and the peace to observe is surprised and feels the void of his own being.

"Let go! Let go!"

The Zen master is talking to his disciple. The disciple is always asking. He wants to know. He wants to be. He wants to have. He wants the teacher to give.

But the master does not give anything.

"So what do I have to let go?" the disciple asks but the master has walked off and isn't listening.

He has to let go of himself. His ideas. Even the insight he thinks he has found. No attainments. Nothing at all. He has to forget his own personality, his own name.

A Chinese allegory tells how a monk sets off on a long pilgrimage to find the Buddha. He spends years and years on his quest and finally he comes to the country where the Buddha lives.

He crosses a river, it is a wide river, and he looks about him while the boatman rows him across.

There is a corpse floating on the water and it is coming closer.

The monk looks. The corpse is so close he can touch it. He recognizes the corpse, it is his own.

The monk loses all self-control and wails.

There he floats, dead.

Nothing remains.

Anything he has ever been, ever learned, ever owned, floats past him, still and without life, moved by the slow current of the wide river.

It is the first moment of his liberation.

About the Author

Born and raised in Amsterdam, Janwillem van de Wetering moved to South Africa when he was nineteen. After living and working there for six years he went to London, where he studied philosophy for a year. From London he went to Kyoto, Japan, and lived in a Zen monastery for the next two years. His travels next took him to Peru and Colombia in South America where he got married and spent three years. From South America he went to Australia for a year and then returned to Amsterdam. He went into business and joined the Amsterdam Reserve Police Force where he swiftly rose through the ranks. Van de Wetering and his wife moved to Maine ten years ago and still make their home there.

He chronicles his Zen experiences in *The Empty Mirror* and *A Glimpse of Nothingness*. Novels in the Amsterdam Cop series include *Outsider in Amsterdam, Tumbleweed, The Corpse on the Dike, Death of a Hawker, The Japanese Corpse, The Blond Baboon, The Maine Massacre, The Mind-Murders, The Streetbird, The Rattle-Rat,* and *Hard Rain. Inspector Saito's Small Satori* introduces us to a new cop, and *The Sergeant's Cat* is a collection of short stories. *Murder by Remote Control* is a mystery told in comic book format.